Doing Business in Korea:

2013 Country Commercial Guide for U.S. Companies

Return to table of contents

Chapter 1: Doing Business In Korea

- Market Overview
- Market Challenges
- Market Opportunities
- Market Entry Strategy
- Market Fact Sheet

Market Overview   Return to top

The long-anticipated Korea-U.S. Free Trade Agreement (KORUS) went into force on March 15, 2012, becoming our nation's largest FTA since NAFTA. The Agreement is expected to increase U.S. exports to Korea by approximately USD 10-12 billion. In 2011, more than 20,000 SMEs exported $13.9 billion in goods to South Korea, a 22% increase from known SME exports in 2010.

Total 2011 U.S.-Korea trade exceeded USD 100 billion for the first time ever, also surpassing that mark in 2012. Total U.S. exports in 2012 exceeded USD 42.3 billion.

Korea is the United States' eighth largest export market. The U.S. is the third largest exporter to Korea, with an 8.3 percent market share of Korea's total imports. Key competitors include China with 15.5 percent, Japan with 12.4 percent, and the EU's 27 nations with 9.7 percent. With the EU having already implemented its FTA with Korea, U.S. firms will now be on more equal footing with the benefit of KORUS implementation. (China's trade reflects significant re-export activity.)

Korea's projected 2013 GDP growth forecast is 2.8%, according to the International Monetary Fund. Its commercial banks maintain strong reserves in the case of a possible global slowdown or difficulties in the Euro Zone.

Korea will continue to focus its development on key economic growth sectors. Patents, trademarks and industrial designs issued by the Korea Intellectual Property Office (KIPO) reached 400,815 in 2012. The increasing trend in local patent and trademark filings reflects the move toward more technology-intensive and capital-intensive industries and services.

Market Challenges   Return to top

Unique industry standards, less than transparent regulations, pressures to reduce prices and 'contract negotiations' continue to affect U.S. business in Korea. However, firms which are innovative, patient, and exhibit a commitment to the Korean market generally continue to find business to be rewarding and Koreans to be loyal customers. With the implementation of KORUS now in process, Korea's attractiveness as a market will continue to improve. U.S. products will become increasingly cost-competitive and bilateral trade should increase. EU products have had reduced or zero-tariff access to this market since mid-2011.

U.S. SMEs must remain flexible and ready to work with their Korean business counterparts as it pertains to *amending contract terms* or renegotiating price, quantity, and delivery terms, following a business deal or bilateral contractual agreement. In Korea, the principal of 'consideration', as is the case in English law, is not present. A request to amend an offer or to restart negotiations with a counteroffer likely will not include any payment for consideration on the Korean side. Koreans feel that the signing of a contract is only the beginning of a business relationship.

U.S. exporters of agricultural commodities also face market challenges related to import regulations and testing requirements. Please see the latest USDA/Agricultural Trade Office (ATO) Korea Export Guide at:
http://gain.fas.usda.gov/Recent%20GAIN%20Publications/Exporter%20Guide_Seoul%2
0ATO_Korea%20-%20Republic%20of_10-29-2012.pdf

Market Opportunities Return to top

The Korean USD 1 trillion economy is heavily-weighted toward international trade. Trade accounts for 90 percent of its GDP. As Korea continues to move toward more technology-intensive industries, U.S. companies will find market opportunities in leading industries such as life sciences (medical devices, pharmaceuticals, and biotechnology), industrial chemicals, IT, nanotechnology, aerospace/defense, energy, environmental technology, and transportation. U.S. companies are already partnering with local Korean industries to expand market opportunities from Korea to third-country markets, including ASEAN, the Middle East, and other markets in the Asia-Pacific region. Given Korea's strong shipping and air cargo infrastructure, this is not only a market for U.S. goods and services, but also a hub for eventual expansion into other markets.

Market Entry Strategy Return to top

- A local presence is essential for success. Retain a manufacturer's representative, distributor, or name a registered trading company as an agent or establish a branch sales office.

- Establishing and maintaining a strong business relationship is essential. Companies should visit Korea frequently to cultivate contacts and to better understand business conditions.

- For marketing support of U.S. agricultural commodities and processed foods, consult:
  http://gain.fas.usda.gov/Recent%20GAIN%20Publications/Exporter%20Guide_Seoul
  %20ATO_Korea%20-%20Republic%20of_10-29-2012.pdf

CS Korea is eager to assist U.S. companies in developing the right connections/contacts in Korea, through a wide range of marketing services designed to identify and arrange introduction to potential buyers, distributors and importers. Consult:
http://export.gov/southkorea/servicesforuscompanies/index.asp

Market Fact Sheet Return to top

COUNTRY FACT SHEET: KOREA, REPUBLIC OF

PROFILE

Population in 2012 (Millions): 51
Capital: Seoul
Government: Republic

ECONOMY	2010	2011	2012
Nominal GDP (Current Billions $U.S.)	1,015	1,116	1,130
Nominal GDP Per Capita (Current $US)	20,540	22,424	22,708
Real GDP Growth Rate (% change)	6.3	3.6	2.1
Real GDP Growth Rate Per Capita (% change)	5.8	2.9	1.6
Consumer Prices (% change)	2.9	4	2.2
Unemployment (% of labor force)	3.7	3.4	3.5

Economic Mix in 2010: 39.3% All Industries; 30.6% Manufactures; 58.2% Services; 2.6% Agriculture

FOREIGN MERCHANDISE TRADE ($US Millions)	2010	2011	2012
Korea, Republic Of Exports to World	466,384	555,214	548,076
Korea, Republic Of Imports from World	425,212	524,413	519,582
U.S. Exports to Korea, Republic Of	38,846	43,415	42,318
U.S. Imports from Korea, Republic Of	48,875	56,661	58,880
U.S. Trade Balance with Korea, Republic Of	-10,029	-13,247	-16,562
Position in U.S. Trade:			
Rank of Korea, Republic Of in U.S. Exports	7	7	8
Rank of Korea, Republic Of in U.S. Imports	7	6	7
Korea, Republic Of Share (%) of U.S. Exports	3	3	2.7
Korea, Republic Of Share (%) of U.S. Imports	3	3	2.6

Principal U.S. Exports to Korea, Republic Of in 2012:

1. Computer & Electronic Products (16.5%)
2. Chemicals (16.4%)
3. Machinery, Except Electrical (14.5%)
4. Transportation Equipment (11.7%)

5. Food & Kindred Products (7.0%)

Principal U.S. Imports from Korea, Republic Of in 2012:

1. Transportation Equipment (28.6%)
2. Computer & Electronic Products (22.8%)
3. Machinery, Except Electrical (8.8%)
4. Primary Metal Mfg (6.8%)
5. Electrical Equipment, Appliances & Components (6.4%)

Foreign Direct Investment	2010	2011	2012
U.S. FDI in Korea, Republic Of (US $Millions)	43,783	46,155	49,829
FDI in U.S. by Korea, Republic Of (US $Millions)	39,262	54,833	62,079

DOING BUSINESS/ECONOMIC FREEDOM RANKINGS

World Bank Doing Business in 2012 Rank: 8 of 185
Heritage/WSJ 2012 Index of Freedom Rank: 31 of 179

Return to table of contents

Return to table of contents

Chapter 2: Political and Economic Environment

For background information on the political and economic environment of the country, please click on the link below to the U.S. Department of State Background Notes.

http://www.state.gov/r/pa/ei/bgn/2800.htm

Return to table of contents

Chapter 3: Selling U.S. Products and Services

- Using an Agent or Distributor
- Establishing an Office
- Franchising
- Direct Marketing
- Joint Ventures (JV) /Licensing
- Selling to the Government
- Distribution and Sales Channels
- Selling Factors/Techniques
- Electronic Commerce
- Trade Promotion and Advertising
- Pricing
- Sales Service/Customer Support
- Protecting Your Intellectual Property
- Due Diligence
- Local Professional Services
- Web Resources

Using an Agent or Distributor   Return to top

Before entering into a contractual relationship with a Korean manufacturers/commission representative (agent) or distributor, U.S. firms should conduct a thorough due diligence on a prospective business partner. A contract with an agent or distributor should be handled with care and with the assistance of an attorney. The Commercial Service in Korea can assist by providing companies with an Individual Company Profile (ICP) (Consult: http://export.gov/southkorea/servicesforuscompanies/icp/index.asp) report, which provides detailed financial and related business information on the company you seek to work with.

The most common means of product or service representation in Korea are:

- Appointing a registered/commissioned agent or "offer agent" on an exclusive or non-exclusive basis;

- Naming a registered trading company as manufacturer's representative or agent; or

- Establishing a branch sales office, managed by home office personnel along with Korean staff.

Additionally:

- Any businessperson registered with the Korean government can import goods in his/her own name.

- A 'registered trading company' can manage all import documentation. These are typically larger firms involved in both exports and imports. However, these firms can be less attentive to building the U.S. supplier's business, even though they can be influential and well-known in the marketplace.

Performance of your agent/distributor should be regularly/frequently monitored. An under-performing or non-performing agent/distributor should be counseled and properly guided. If, after a period of time, performance is still poor (and only after careful consideration of all legal and contractual obligations), a termination of contract should be considered. Once a termination is legally binding, the U.S. firm should begin searching for a new distributor.

Finding a Good Partner in Korea

The U.S. Dept. of Commerce's Commercial Service (CS) office in Seoul, like CS offices around the world, offers the Gold Key Service (GKS) (See: http://export.gov/southkorea/servicesforuscompanies/gks/index.asp) to assist U.S. companies in finding a good partner in Korea.

U.S. exporters are urged to contact one of over 100 U.S. Export Assistance Centers (USEACs; please contact the USEAC closest to your business). Consult: http://export.gov/usoffices/index.asp to begin the process.

The GKS provides:

- A customized schedule of face-to-face meetings with carefully-selected prospective candidates;

- A briefing, interpretation service, and transportation (fee based); and

- Information regarding each meeting, focused market research, and insights gained by CS specialists in the process of setting-up the GKS.

CS Korea strongly recommends that:

- U.S. companies seek legal counsel prior to signing a contract or making major business decisions with Korean companies.

- Any distribution or agency contract should include a termination clause. If not, Korean commercial arbitration bodies may specify the terms for termination, including compensation claims against the principal. A mutually-signed contract between a supplier and an agent/distributor, with termination provisions, would take precedence and avoid placing the U.S. company at risk.

- U.S. companies should protect their intellectual property, trademark and patents with the Korean Intellectual Property Office (KIPO). Consult: http://www.kipo.go.kr/kpo/user.tdf?a=user.english.main.BoardApp&c=1001) as a minimum safeguard of your intellectual property rights.

- A local Korean or U.S. attorney in Korea can easily perform these tasks. Under Korean law, applications to KIPO must be competed and submitted in Korean. This should be done in the U.S. company's name and not the Korean agent/representative's name. Since the passage of the KORUS FTA, there are now numerous large U.S. law firms with offices in Korea. Additionally, there are some 14,000 Korean lawyers practicing in Korea.

Establishing an Office

The dynamism and maturity of the Korean market, coupled with its strategic location in East Asia, may lead U.S. companies to consider opening an office in Korea. The following options exist:

- **Subsidiary Office:** Established as a local company, a subsidiary has a closer relationship with the local business community and can provide the local firm the opportunity for Korean government investment incentives, as it would be eligible to receive corporate income tax incentives (Special Tax Treatment Law STTCL), if it meets certain requirements. These tax incentives are not available to branch or liaison offices.

- **Branch Office:** Not subject to audits by external auditors in Korea, a branch office's net income is automatically viewed as being included in the headquarters balance sheet. A company expecting to grow large enough to require the establishment of a subsidiary in the future should consider doing so from the beginning, rather than starting as a branch operation.

- **Liaison Office:** A liaison office can only conduct marketing and support and cannot conduct direct sales. A liaison office is subject only to the tax code of the headquarters country and is the simplest form of conducting business in Korea.

Basic guidelines to setting-up an office in Korea include:

- Review *Invest KOREA:* Consult the one-stop services offered by Invest KOREA (Consult: http://www.investkorea.org/InvestKoreaWar/work/ik/eng/) a government-sponsored, non-profit organization of the Korea Trade-Investment Promotion Agency (KOTRA; http://english.kotra.or.kr/wps/portal/dken).

- KOTRA maintains offices throughout the United States, poised to guide U.S. companies through the administrative, legal and tax implications of opening an office in Korea. KOTRA also has an 'investment ombudsman' ready to quickly address foreign investors' grievances. Consult: http://www.investkorea.org/InvestKoreaWar/work/ombsman/eng/au/index.jsp?num=3

- *Authorization:* Once 'authorization to proceed' with an investment is granted, companies must notify the Ministry of Trade, Industry and Energy (MOTIE), a delegated authority (major Korean bank), or Invest Korea. Consult: http://www.investkorea.org/InvestKoreaWar/work/ik/eng/

- *Your Office in Korea:* Consult a reputable real estate agent or real estate consulting firm when deciding on the best location for your office. A partial list is available at:

http://export.gov/southkorea/usefullinks/majorrealestateaccountinghrfirmsinkorea/index.asp

- Under Korea's Foreign Land Acquisition Law, foreigners can purchase land regardless of size or purpose. Local zoning laws regulate categories of activity allowed and should be reviewed prior to making final investment decisions.

- *Register with the Tax Office:* Investors must register their office/investment with the local tax office. Given language issues, the complexity of Korean tax laws, and the potential for misunderstanding, companies should hire a local accounting firm to file taxes. Consult:
http://export.gov/southkorea/usefullinks/majorrealestateaccountinghrfirmsinkorea/index.asp

- *Seek Qualified Employees:* Koreans are attracted to U.S. firms, given salary rates, prestige, opportunities for travel, the ability to use and learn English, and the possibility to transfer to the company's home office or another foreign branch office.

    Korea has a large pool of conscientious and highly-educated workers. Female employees are especially strong candidates, given their educational achievements, language abilities, and the prevalence of traditional Korean cultural attitudes toward female employees (which have historically prevented them from progressing as quickly as they would in a U.S. company).

    Due to differences in U.S. and Korean employment practices, CS Korea recommends consulting Korean employment agencies before hiring.

- Contact the *Seoul Global Center* website for Seoul Metropolitan Government's program which occasionally offers free or reduced rent/office space for foreign residents (http://global.seoul.go.kr/).

Franchising   Return to top

The franchise market in 2012 was valued at an estimated USD 84.3 billion (franchise, sub-franchise fees and royalties, product and service revenues, consulting fees, related product sales and equipment; Ministry of Trade, Industry and Energy).

Nearly 3,034 franchises were registered in Korea in 2011. Some 1,240,000 employees are currently working in this industry. There are some 21,121 convenience store franchises operating in Korea (*2012 Yearbook of Retail Industry),* of which 5,085 opened in 2011. Nearly 2,145 were food service franchises, 276 were retail franchises, and 613 were service franchises. On average, a franchise operates 68.5 stores across its industry in Korea.

Franchisors interested in this market must:

- Meet the rules promulgated under: Korea's Fair Transactions in Franchise Business Act, and the new regulations pending implementation from National Commission for Corporate Partnership (NCCP);

- Be registered with the Korea Fair Trade Commission; and

- Comply with the sub-franchisee's Fair Trade Act, which stipulates the need for disclosure of all business information to potential sub-franchisees at least 14 days before signing an agreement. This Act closely parallels the rules that exist for sub-franchisees in the U.S.

The Korea-U.S. FTA (KORUS) will positively affect this industry in many ways, to include:

- Expedited Customs Procedures: Improved transparency through the publication of customs measures will ensure U.S. companies have access to customs laws and regulations. In addition, the Agreement requires simplified customs procedures for timely and efficient release of goods.

- Protected U.S. Investment: A stable, legal framework will protect all forms of U.S. investment. The KORUS FTA promises U.S. investors national treatment, which means they will be treated equally to Korean investors in the establishment, acquisition, and operation of their investments in Korea.

In 2012, Korea's large retail players reported interest in opening numerous mega malls outside the Seoul metropolitan area, over the next three to five years. These highly respected (mostly *Chaebol*) retailers seek retail anchor stores, franchise food service establishments and restaurants with a unique concept or theme for their expansion projects. Several companies are interested in becoming master franchisors of U.S. franchise brands, as well as wanting U.S. franchise tenants for their new malls/stores.

Opportunities exist for franchises in: wellness/well-being, environmentally friendly products, sports and leisure activities, personal service, green growth, children's services, education, laundry service, auto maintenance, hair care, senior day care, homecare, home delivery services (all sectors), home child care, human resource training and pet service, to name a few.

Korean franchisees are reluctant to pay the high franchising fees (USD 90,000 to 180,000) and royalties often required by U.S. companies. Domestic chains are popular because they do not require much capital or large royalty fee payments.

Minimum facility size and number of store openings required by U.S. franchisors are also a challenge for the Korean franchisee. The unique and expensive nature of the commercial real estate sector in Korea can affect the feasibility of a project which may otherwise offer great promise in other markets.

Korean franchisees prefer to do business with U.S. franchisors that offer established brand names to Korean consumers, as well as offering American-style, systematic operations and management skills.

There are three basic types of franchise investors in Korea:

- Investors with little or no experience in the franchise they seek to own/start;

- Individuals with real experience with franchising brands; and

- "Retirees" with a strong business background, but who have downsized (age 40 and above) and wish to own their own business.

U.S. investors should seek an experienced workforce which they can mentor and monitor in this mature market.

As part of Korea's efforts in 2012 and into 2013 to bring about economic democratization, the National Commission for Corporate Partnership (NCCP) recommended that regulations be imposed on large companies/conglomerates to provide opportunities and raise the competitiveness of SMEs in the franchise sector. The NCCP classifies large companies/conglomerates as those with annual sales over 20 billion won, with more than 200 employees, under the Minor Enterprise Basic Law. A whole series of restrictions, such as denying a conglomerate the ability to open a new store located less than 500 meters from an existing shop of the same brand, is scheduled to go into force in 2013. At present, there are no exceptions for foreign companies operating in Korea, if their annual sales are over 20 billion won and with more than 200 employees.

The NCCP's new regulations will be in effect for approximately three years, from approximately May 2013 to March 2016. Franchise brands must follow these rules or will be penalized with fines imposed by Korea's Small and Medium Business Administration (KSMBA). At this writing, with the regulations still in draft form, it is assumed that about 30 companies (Chaebols) will be affected by these regulations or semi-official rules. Chaebols are already proving unwilling to 'rock-the-boat' in reference to these regulations.

While the effects of economic democratization and the NCCP's new regulations will indeed have a dampening effect on U.S. franchisors, opportunities do exist in Korea's nearly half-dozen new cities or communities which are growing and gaining momentum. In this case, U.S. franchises would need to make their own investments in these new cities, for a two-to-four year period, until a Korean master franchisee is identified and/or until the NCCP regulations expire.

Direct Marketing Return to top

The 2012 Retail Industry Yearbook indicates that the online shopping industry is consistently growing and was estimated to be USD 39.9 billion (US 1$=KRW 1,126.28). This is a 15 percent increase from 2011 (USD 35.1 billion, US 1$=KRW 1,126.28). Direct marketing primarily takes the form of catalog sales, TV home shopping, internet shopping, and the mobile commerce market. Korea also has a large market for door-to-door sales, as well as a robust multi-level marketing sector. Internet sales account for nearly 80 percent of all sales among the four direct sales channels (catalog sales, TV home shopping, internet shopping, and mobile commerce). U.S. companies are encouraged to take seriously all four sales channels in this highly consumer-oriented market.

Door-to-Door Sales

The major door-to-door sales items include home education materials, books, household consumer goods, cosmetics, health food, sporting goods, and services (such as insurance). According to the Korea Direct Selling Association (KDSA: http://www.kdsa.or.kr/), the Korean door-to-door sales market was approximately USD 7.3 billion (US 1$=KRW 1,126.28) in 2011.

Multi-Level Marketing (MLM)

Korea's multi-level marketing sales for 2011 approached USD 2.5 billion (US 1$=KRW 1,126.28). Nearly 100 registered multi-level marketing companies employed about 4 million active distributors.

The Korean government reduced restrictions on MLM companies by passing legislation eliminating most existing market barriers against MLM products, such as the obligation to disclose retail prices on the MLM product label. Oversight of the MLM industry is the responsibility of the Korean Fair Trade Commission (FTC).

MLM activities by U.S. firms in the cosmetics, cleaning products, and kitchenware industries have been expanding. MLM activities by U.S. firms within these sectors should promote their products and services appropriately and efficiently by analyzing Korean market trends. Knowledge of the market can prevent unnecessary conflicts with government agencies, consumer 'watchdog' groups, or industry groups.

Joint Ventures (JVs) / Licensing   Return to top

Koreans prefer to maintain local control of JV operations with foreign entities. Thus, the financial goals, internal organization and key management issues of a JV must be agreed upon by all involved parties as early as possible.

Foreign direct investment (FDI) is encouraged and promoted by the Korean government. With the ratification and implementation of the KORUS FTA, greater cooperation and encouragement of FDI is expected.

When considering FDI in Korea, it is important to consider the following:

- The decreasing influence of (some) *chaebols*, the Korean government's promotion of SMEs, the government's interest in seeking anti-monopolistic and more diversified JVs;

- Koreans prefer to maintain local control, regardless of the percentage invested by foreign entities; and

- Management control should be evaluated on three levels: 1) shareholder equity; 2) representation on the board of directors; and 3) active management (representative director and subordinate management). Legally, Korean board meetings require the physical presence of all JV members, as well as a quorum of the directors. If a foreign investor intends to exercise day-to-day management of an operation, a representative director who resides in Korea must be appointed. The director requires the support of and access to key functional areas of the company in order to manage in accordance with the foreign investor's wishes.

Contractual Agreements in Korea

Well-written, well-understood, and well-executed contractual agreements are the basis and backbone to a U.S. firm's success in Korea. Cultural differences surrounding the expectations of a contractual agreement and how one successfully arrives at a mutually beneficial agreement is often the basis of consternation and challenges.

For Koreans:

- A contract represents the 'current understanding' of a deal. It is the beginning, rather than the end, to a negotiation;
- Any change in the contract (omissions, invalid issues, new leadership, non-existent issues) may cause problems to arise;
- Koreans may regard a contract as a "gentlemen's agreement" subject to further negotiation *should conditions change*; Americans generally regard the same written agreement as legally binding.

Contract negotiations in Korea must be viewed as an *on-going process of dialogue* and should have the following objectives:

- Reaching a common understanding about the deal/contract
- Reaching an understanding about each party's responsibilities
- Recording the detailed understandings
- Being *prepared to modify the terms of the agreement should there be a change* in circumstances (leadership, other issues).

Additionally, the following precautions should be addressed:

- Technology transfer, raw material supplies, marketing, and distribution should be agreed upon, in detail, in the JV agreement

- A company's IP may not be protected and could be vulnerable in the later stages of a JV business relationship, especially if the Korean company depends upon transfer of technology (see Protecting your IP, also in this chapter).

- Korea's legal system can be lengthy, cumbersome and expensive. When dealing with contracts, the best strategy is to prevent conflicts.

- Foreign investors should consult the Korean Commercial Arbitration Board (Consult: http://www.kcab.or.kr/servlet/kcab_adm/memberauth/5000). The KCAB advises foreign companies on contract guidelines.

Selling to the Government   Return to top

Government Procurement

Korea is an established member of the World Trade Organization's Government Procurement Agency (GPA) protocols, establishing non-discriminatory government procurement procedures.

Korea's GPA commitments include:

- "Threshold" amounts by certain Korean government agencies and provincial authorities
- Procurement commitments in the services and construction industries
- A prohibition against offsets as a condition for awarding contracts
- A provision allowing suppliers to pursue alleged violations through GPA-defined bid challenge procedures
- An International Contract Dispute Settlement Committee
- Annexes specifying certain thresholds below which GPA rules do not apply (approximately USD 180,000 and, for construction services, approximately USD 7 million)
- Korea is exempted from GPA coverage for items related to national security and defense, procurement of satellites, and purchases by the Korea Electric Power Corporation (KEPCO: http://www.kepco.co.kr/eng/) of certain electrical transmission and distribution equipment.

U.S. companies interested in Korean government procurement must also work with Korea's Public Procurement Service (PPS). Consult: http://www.pps.go.kr/english/.

The PPS supports domestic equipment and supplies and is responsible for the purchase of goods and incidental services required by central and sub-central government entities, government construction contracts and the stockpiling of raw materials.

Bidders must register with PPS one business day prior to the date of an opening bid. Foreign bidders can register with PPS (Korean language only) prior to entering into a contract. Failure to register constitutes cause for rejection of the bid.

Korea has launched its Government e-Procurement System (GePS) at http://www.pps.go.kr/english/. In part, the system includes:

- A single window for public procurement, showing the entire process
- Bids which are valid at least 45 days
- Bids must be published with a summary in English, including the subject matter of the contract, the deadline for submission of tenders, and the address and contact point from which full documents relating to the contracts may be obtained
- The complete procurement process, with specifications and requirements (biases against imported products and services are rarely overt; if they occur, these should be brought to the attention of the U.S. Embassy).

The newly-minted KORUS FTA, in effect since March 15, 2012, has a chapter devoted to government procurement. Consult: http://www.ustr.gov/.

Defense Procurement

Defense procurement is an active part of CS Korea's portfolio. U.S. companies which sell to foreign and U.S. militaries should be cognizant of the importance given to military procurement on the Korean peninsula.

The Defense Acquisition Program Administration (DAPA: http://www.dapa.go.kr/eng/index.jsp) is responsible for Korean defense procurement and was established to ensure transparency in defense procurement. DAPA consolidates eight procurement and technology development organizations under the Ministry of National Defense (MND: www.mnd.go.kr/mndEng/main/index.jsp) and various military services. Although a civilian agency under the authority of the Executive Office of the President of Korea, DAPA works directly with the Minister of Defense and the service branches.

U.S. defense industry equipment standards are accepted in Korea as most Korean defense systems are based on American standards. Interoperability of systems is critical in what is now a sixty-year U.S./ROK defense partnership.

Defense equipment is marketed by direct purchase, sales agents, and importer channels. U.S. manufacturers/suppliers of defense equipment should use a well-qualified/vetted Korean agent who is familiar with the ROK defense system and also knowledgeable of key members of the country's Air Force (ROKAF), Navy (ROKN), Army (ROKA), and Agency for Defense Development (ADD). Former ROKAF, ROKN, and ROK A officials have good potential as commissioned representatives in Korea. Local representatives must register and be certified by DAPA to supply their products and services to the MND.

In 2011 the Korean Importers Association (KOIMA: http://www.import.or.kr/) became DAPA's sole source for legacy supplies and parts.

A well-selected representative can provide U.S. suppliers with information about the status of defense bids and procurement plans. Companies wanting to supply their products/systems to DAPA are required to register with this agency, typically a 10-day process. Consult: https://www.d2b.go.kr/English/jsp/regi/HI_HPD_E_regi_Main.jsp?md=311&cfn=HI_HPD_E_regi_01.

Distribution and Sales Channels   Return to top

South Korea is 70 percent mountains, forcing it's nearly 50 million people into key population centers: Seoul metro area: 11 million; Busan metro area: 4 million; Daegu metro area: 3 million; and Daejeon metro area: 2 million. Most freight forwarders use an extensive network of first-class railways, 3,000 kilometers of highways, and air routes that crisscross the country.

Incheon, Gimpo, and Busan's first class airports and ports are the points of entry for most products. Products are then transferred by first-tier roads and railways to major modern distribution centers in Seoul, Busan, Incheon, Daegu, and Gwangyang. South Korea has eight international airports and seven domestic airports, including the world-class Incheon International Airport. Around 77 international passenger and cargo airlines operate frequent flights between Korea and many nations around the world.

Distribution methods and the function of intermediaries vary widely by product in this mature market. Traditional retail distribution networks of small family-run stores, stalls in markets, and street vendors are being replaced by large discount stores.

As part of Korea's efforts to protect small "mom-and-pop" stores, under the auspices of "economic democratization," in mid-2012 the government imposed a rule closing big-box discount chains on Sunday. The U.S. Costco (Korea being one of Costco's most lucrative markets) and other retailers initially ignored the restriction. The government then imposed financial penalties on Costco and other discount stores, which eventually began complying by closing its stores on the second and fourth Sunday of each month in late 2012.

Korea's major cities have numerous fashionable and expensive large department stores and boutiques. Thousands of second-tier and third-tier retail stores also abound. Full-Line Discount Stores (FDS) have gained popularity, as have U.S.-based Costco, which entered the Korean FDS market more than 10 years ago and is successfully competing against Korean rivals E-mart and Lotte Mart.

Rapid expansion of discount chain stores is planned nationwide, with suburban satellite cities attracting the greatest number of stores. Distribution of goods through large discount chains is one of the best ways to market foreign products to Korean consumers.

It should also be noted that parallel imports can legally enter Korea. Many U.S. companies continue to give exclusive contracts, since territorial limits in neighboring countries enhance the value of an exclusive area in any one country. Any parallel importer in Korea not receiving the support of the OEM, and which does not deal in a meaningful volume, cannot be guaranteed a steady source of supply. The legitimate exclusive distributor still has considerable advantages in Korea.

A handful of Korea's highly successful and sophisticated retailers have called CS Korea over the past 12 months, seeking introductions to U.S. name-brand retailers and anchor stores for their three- to five-year mall construction plans.

Selling Factors/Techniques Return to top

Korea is a country with intense, demanding and eager consumers. U.S. companies wanting to sell into this market should endeavor to follow these guidelines:

- Adapt company products and procedures to Korean tastes and conditions
- Communicate regularly with both your Korean business partner and customers
- Exhibit a consistent, firm and long-term commitment to the Korean market
- Work at building long-term relationships
- Augment the efforts of your local representative by visiting Korea frequently
- Invite Korean representatives back to the home office periodically to ensure they are fully informed, motivated, and up-to-date on your company and its offerings
- To the extent possible, allow the distributor/agent to select from all of the U.S. company's product lines
- Hold demonstrations, seminars and exhibitions of products in Korea
- Increase the distribution of technical data and descriptive brochures
- Assist local representatives with follow-up on sales leads.

Electronic Commerce Return to top

E-Commerce is a key component of the overall consumer market in Korea, a country where 98 percent of its population (15 million households) is connected to the web, making e-commerce a key component of Korea's overall consumer market (also see the previous section on Direct Marketing). Characteristics of e-commerce in Korea include:

- Over 30,000 B2C Korean cyber shopping malls in Korea
- B2B, B2G, B2C and C2C transactions in 2009 accounted for 88.2, 8.8, 1.8 and 1.2 percent of the e-commerce sector, respectively
- Major factors driving growth include national broadband infrastructure, with 37 million internet users, and the introduction of 4G Long Term Evolution (LTE), Wireless Broadband (WiBro), as well as wide coverage of WiFi services utilized by mobile computers and smart communication devices
- New social commerce services, led by local companies like Ticket Monster, We Make Price, One a Day, etcetera, spur demand for e-commerce solutions: the equipment, networking, software and services
- Manufacturing industries account for 68 percent of all B2B transactions and these same industries are investing in order to have reliable, efficient and secure e-commerce tools
- U.S. based e-commerce companies should review the Personal Information Protection Act and ministerial data privacy/spam regulations (2007), which may restrict e-commerce for firms managing user-data on international servers.

Trade Promotion and Advertising   Return to top

The U.S. Department of Commerce's (USDOC) International Trade Administration (ITA) and the Commercial Service (CS) office in the U.S. Embassy in Seoul is the U.S. Government's primary trade promotion agency. Consult: http://www.export.gov/southkorea.

In Korea, the Commercial Service works with numerous trading and commercial entities, to include:

- The Korea International Trade Association (KITA): http://www.kita.org/. KITA organizes trade missions, conducts market surveys, assists potential foreign buyers or sellers, and offers consultation and personalized advisory services regarding trade rules and regulations, export and import procedures, business management, market research, technology development and taxation. KITA has offices in Washington, DC and New York.

- The Korean Chamber of Commerce and Industry (KCCI): http://english.korcham.net/. KCCI is Korea's largest private economic organization, with 71 regional chambers and approximately 135,000 members. Since its establishment in 1884, KCCI has contributed to the growth and development of the national economy and also to the enhancement of Korea's status in the international community.

- The Korean Importers Association (KOIMA): http://www.import.or.kr/. KOIMA is Korea's primary importers association and represents over 8,000 businesses.

Korea hosts many trade shows and exhibitions each year. Historically, many of these shows are highly focused on B2C activities and, thus, are not necessarily attractive to U.S. firms interested in meeting qualified companies, versus end-users. The following trade facilities and event schedules may be of interest to U.S. firms:

- COEX: http://coex.co.kr/eng/index.asp - Korea's largest full-service trade show organization, has 36,027 square meters of exhibition space. Hundreds of shows (B2B and B2C) are held throughout the year.

- SETEC: http://www.setec.or.kr/main.do - The Seoul Trade Exhibition Center is operated by the Korea Trade-Investment Promotion Agency (KOTRA).

- KINTEX: http://www.kintex.com/client/_eng/index.jsp

- BEXCO: http://www.bexco.co.kr/ - Located in Busan, Korea's second largest city (southeast Korea), BEXCO holds dozens of B2C and B2B national exhibitions and features 26,446 square meters of exhibition space.

Advertising

A geographically small country, Korea is an exciting place to launch effective, sophisticated, state-of-the-art advertising. Korean advertisers are highly creative and utilize a host of media to capture the consumer's attention.

Particular aspects of Korea's advertising market include:

- More than 80 mega-LED screens strategically pepper commercial areas (in Seoul and other cities) with 24/7 promotions. Monthly advertising opportunities exist.

- Thousands of excellent promotional sites on Korea's well-used bus stops, subway stations, railways and airports should be considered by U.S. firms

- The presence of over 495 foreign (to include all major ad agencies) and Korean ad agencies. Foreign equity participation is permitted at 100 percent.

- Hundreds of TV and radio stations, consisting of:
    - KBS I, KBS II: TV and radio owned/operated by the Korean government
    - MBC, SBS: Independently operated, but with ROK government influence
    Consult: www.kobaco.co.kr/eng/index.asp

- The Korea Advertising Review Board (KARB: www.kobaco.co.kr/eng/business/publication.asp) is responsible for advertising censorship and the Korean Fair Trade Commission (KFTC) (http://eng.ftc.go.kr/) assures accuracy in advertisement

- The Korean cable TV industry serves 12 million households, with 94 system operators offering over 150 programs. Korea Digital Broadcasting (KDB), a subsidiary of Korea Telecom (KT) (http://www.kt.com/eng/) broadcasts more than150 satellite channels to over three million households.

- Five popular shopping channels (CJ, Hyundai, GS, Lotte, and Nongsusan) grossed over USD 3.5 billion in 2009

Internet advertising offers significant market growth potential. Currently 15 million households, or 98 percent of all households, use the internet.

Pricing Return to top

In Korea's export-driven, raw-material dependent economy, price competitiveness is a serious driver. Korean manufacturers believe it essential to buy the lowest-priced raw materials or equipment, even at the expense of quality. Manufacturers often offset labor costs with low-cost inputs. Japanese goods are considered to be 'better buys.'

Korean buyers generally believe that U.S. goods:

- Have an *overall* good reputation
- Are of high quality and good-to-excellent performance
- Are very expensive.

Pricing in Korea:

- Is dependent upon consumer-protection legislation, which requires that consumer items be labeled with the manufacturer's sales price (to the retailer) and the marked-up retailer's price (to the consumer)
- Ranges from 50 to 150 percent (from the manufacturer to the consumer)
- Include a 10 percent sales tax for taxable items
- Include a 10 percent VAT on services
- Is often dependent on 'bundling'
- Is often undervalued for software, engineering and other services
- Price quotes should take into account price the likelihood of repeat business for spare parts and auxiliary equipment.

Commissions in Korea are dependent upon the type of product and the transaction amount:

- 10 percent (average) for 'spot-basis' transactions
- 5-7 percent for general machinery, packaging, construction and material handling equipment
- 15-18 percent for sophisticated products, i.e., medical, laboratory, and scientific analytical instruments and for products where after-sales service is considered to be very important.

For larger contracts, commissions generally decline as the contract value for a major purchase/acquisition/contract increases.

Sales Service/Customer Support Return to top

Considered secondary to product and price considerations, after-sales service in Korea is often found lacking. A carryover from pre-Korean War times, Koreans often use improvisation and/or expect self-reliance when handling service issues. This should be managed closely, especially given the competition of third countries in this market. Servicing is/should be an important component of the 'sale.'

The best approaches to after-sales service and customer support include:

- Resident or offshore engineers (Japan or Taiwan) working with local engineers; service contracts should be considered
- Establishing a regional servicing facility which can effectively service and support equipment sold in Korea
- Training service and customer service personnel via U.S.-based programs.

Protecting Your Intellectual Property Return to top

Introduction on Intellectual Property Rights in Korea

In Korea, registration of patents and trademarks is on a <u>first-in-time, first-in-right basis</u>. Consider applying for trademark and patent protection <u>before</u> selling your products or services in Korea.

For U.S. small- and medium-size companies, the U.S. Department of Commerce provides one hour of free legal advice via the "SME IP Advisory Program" of the American Bar Association. Consult: http://apps.americanbar.org/intlaw/intlproj/iprprogram_consultation.html.

Protecting Your Intellectual Property in the Republic of Korea

Several general principles are important for effective management of intellectual property (IP) rights in Korea. First, it is important to have an overall strategy to protect your IP. Second, IP is protected differently in the Korean market than in the U.S. Third, rights must be registered and enforced in Korea, under local laws.

Your U.S. trademark and patent registrations will not protect you in the Korean market. There is no such thing as an "international copyright" that will automatically protect an author's writings throughout the entire world. Protection against unauthorized use in a particular country depends, basically, on the national laws of that country. However, most countries do offer copyright protection to foreign works under certain conditions, and these conditions have been greatly simplified by international copyright treaties and conventions.

Registration of patents and trademarks is on a first-in-time, first-in-right basis, so you should consider applying for trademark and patent protection even before selling your products or services in the Korean market. It is vital that companies understand that intellectual property is primarily a private right and that the U.S. government generally cannot enforce rights for private individuals in Korea. It is the responsibility of the rights holders to register, protect, and enforce their rights where relevant, retaining their own counsel and advisors. Companies may wish to seek advice from local attorneys or IP consultants expert in Korean IPR law. The U.S. Commercial Service can provide a list of local lawyers upon request. Please consult: http://export.gov/southkorea/usefullinks/lawfirms/index.asp.

While the U.S. Government stands ready to assist, there is little that can be done if rights holders have not taken the fundamental steps necessary to secure and enforce their IP in a timely fashion. Moreover, in many countries, rights holders who delay enforcing rights in a mistaken belief that the USG can provide a political resolution to a legal problem may find that their rights have been eroded or abrogated due to legal doctrines such as statutes of limitation, laches, estoppel, or unreasonable delay in prosecuting a law suit. In no instance should U.S. Government advice be seen as a substitute for the obligation of a rights holder to promptly pursue its case.

It is always advisable to conduct due diligence on potential partners. Negotiate from the position of your partner and give your partner clear incentives to honor the contract. A good partner is an important ally in protecting IP rights. Consider carefully, however, whether to permit your partner to register your IP rights on your behalf. Doing so may create a risk that your partner will list himself as the IP owner and fail to transfer the rights should the partnership end. Keep an eye on your cost structure and reduce the margins (and incentive) of would-be bad actors. Projects and sales in Korea require constant attention. Work with legal counsel familiar with Korean law to create a solid contract that includes non-compete clauses and confidentiality/non-disclosure provisions.

It is also recommended that small- and medium-size companies understand the importance of working with trade associations and other organizations to support efforts to protect IP and stop counterfeiting. There are a number of these organizations, both Korea-based and U.S.-based. These include:

- The U.S. Chamber and local American Chambers of Commerce ("AmChams")
- The National Association of Manufacturers (NAM)
- The International Intellectual Property Alliance (IIPA)
- The International Trademark Association (INTA)
- The Coalition Against Counterfeiting and Piracy
- The International Anti-Counterfeiting Coalition (IACC)
- The Pharmaceutical Research and Manufacturers of America (PhRMA)
- The Biotechnology Industry Organization (BIO)

IP Resources

A wealth of information on protecting IP is freely available to U.S. rights holders. Some excellent resources for companies regarding intellectual property include the following:

- For information about patent, trademark, or copyright issues -- including enforcement issues in the U.S. and other countries -- call the STOP! Hotline: 1-866-999-HALT or register at http://www.stopfakes.gov/

- For more information about registering trademarks and patents (both in the U.S. as well as in foreign countries), contact the U.S. Patent and Trademark Office (USPTO) at: 1-800-786-9199

- For more information about registering for copyright protection in the U.S., contact the U.S. Copyright Office at 1-202-707-5959.

- For more information about how to evaluate, protect, and enforce intellectual property rights and how these rights may be important for businesses, a free on-line training program is available at http://www.stopfakes.gov/data/us/menu/index.htm

- For U.S. small- and medium-size companies, the U.S. Department of Commerce offers its "SME IP Advisory Program" through the American Bar Association, which provides one hour of free IP legal advice for companies with concerns in Brazil, China, Egypt, India, Russia, and other markets. For details and to register, visit: http://www.abanet.org/intlaw/intlproj/iprprogram_consultation.html.

- For information on obtaining and enforcing intellectual property rights and for a market-specific IP Toolkit for Korea visit: http://export.gov/southkorea/iprtoolkit/index.asp, as linked from www.StopFakes.gov. This site is linked to the USPTO website for registering trademarks and patents (both in the U.S. as well as in foreign countries), as well as the U.S. Customs & Border Protection website to record registered trademarks and copyrighted works and allows you to register for webinars on protecting IP.

Due Diligence Return to top

Conducting a thorough due diligence check is critical when selecting a local partner for a JV, licensing, and distribution. A due diligence check should include:

- An evaluation of the company's financial and operational history
- Accounting practices
- Hidden ownership interests
- Corporate relationships with other Korean companies
- Position in the market for the product(s) you are exporting

CS Korea offers a fee-based service called the International Country Profile (ICP): http://export.gov/southkorea/servicesforuscompanies/icp/index.asp. The ICP includes the above information, obtained by the Commercial Service in Korea, in addition to a visit the office of the Korean company as well as obtaining financial information from D&B Korea Co., Ltd. (http://www.dnbasia.com/kr/english/sitemap/) and Kroll International (http://www.kroll.com/), both of which also provide due diligence reports.

Local Professional Services Return to top

Korea has a highly developed economy with a full range of professional services:

Agents/distributors: http://export.gov/southkorea/usefullinks/usefulcontactsregardingagentsdistributors/index.asp

Law firms: http://export.gov/southkorea/usefullinks/lawfirms/index.asp

Major banks: http://export.gov/southkorea/usefullinks/majoruskoreanbanks/index.asp

Major real estate and real estate consultancy firms, accounting companies and human resources firms: http://export.gov/southkorea/usefullinks/majorrealestateaccountinghrfirmsinkorea/index.asp

Major newspaper contacts:
http://export.gov/southkorea/usefullinks/majornewspapersbusinessjournals/index.asp

The "Featured U.S. Exporters" (FUSE) site provides information on how you can advertise products on our worldwide website, in various languages, for a small fee. Click http://export.gov/southkorea/bsp/index.asp for more information.

Web Resources   Return to top

Busan Exhibition and Convention Center (BEXCO):
http://www.bexco.co.kr/english/main/main.jsp

Agents or Distributors in Korea:
http://export.gov/southkorea/usefullinks/usefulcontactsregardingagentsdistributors/index.asp

Banks in Korea:
http://export.gov/southkorea/usefullinks/majoruskoreanbanks/index.asp

Convention and Exhibition Center (COEX):
http://coex.co.kr/eng/index.asp

Daegu Exhibition and Convention Center (EXCO Daegu):
http://www.excodaegu.com/

Defense Acquisition and Procurement Agency (DAPA):
http://www.dapa.go.kr/eng/index.jsp

Dun & Bradstreet Korea
http://www.dnbasia.com/kr/english/sitemap/

Featured U.S. Exporters (FUSE)
http://export.gov/southkorea/bsp/index.asp

Government e-Procurement Service (GePS):
http://www.pps.go.kr/english/

International Company Profile:
http://export.gov/southkorea/servicesforuscompanies/icp/index.asp

Invest KOREA:
http://www.investkorea.org/

KITA New York Office:
http://www.kita.net/ny/eng/01/index.html

KITA Washington Office:
http://www.kita.net/ny/eng/02/index.html

Korea Broadcast Advertising Corporation (KOBACO):
http://www.kobaco.co.kr/eng/index.asp

Korean Commercial Arbitration Board:
http://www.kcab.or.kr/servlet/kcab_adm/memberauth/5000

Korea Importer's Association (KOIMA)
http://www.import.or.kr/

Korea Intellectual Property Office (KIPO):
http://www.kipo.go.kr/kpo/user.tdf?a=user.english.main.BoardApp&c=1001

Korea's Main Distribution Centers:
　　Busan: http://busanpa.com/Service.do?id=engmain
　　Daegu: http://english.daegu.go.kr
　　Gwangyang: http://www.gwangyang.go.kr/02en/
　　Incheon: http://www.incheon.go.kr/icweb/html/web39/039.html

Korea Trade Investment Promotion Agency (KOTRA):
http://english.kotra.or.kr/wps/portal/dken

KINTEX
http://www.kintex.com/client/_eng/index.jsp

Kroll Korea:
http://www.krollworldwide.com/

Public Procurement Service (PPS):
http://www.pps.go.kr/english/

Law Firms in Korea:
http://export.gov/southkorea/usefullinks/lawfirms/index.asp

Newspaper Agencies in Korea:
http://export.gov/southkorea/usefullinks/majornewspapersbusinessjournals/index.asp

Real Estate Consultants, Accounting Firms and Human Resource Agencies:
http://export.gov/southkorea/usefullinks/majorrealestateaccountinghrfirmsinkorea/index.asp

Seoul Trade Exhibition Center (SETEC)
http://www.setec.or.kr/main.do

World Federation of Direct Selling Associations
http://www.wfdsa.org/

Return to table of contents

Chapter 4: Leading Sectors for U.S. Export and Investment

Commercial Sectors

- Aerospace Industry
- Cosmetics
- Defense Industry Equipment
- Education Services
- Energy: New and Renewable (NRE)
- Entertainment and Media
- Franchising
- Laboratory Scientific Instruments
- Medical Equipment and Devices
- Pollution Control Equipment
- Semiconductors
- Travel and Tourism

Agricultural Sectors

- Agricultural Sectors

Aerospace Industry

ITA CODE: PR AIR

Overview   Return to top

	2010	2011	2012	2013 (Est.)
Total Market Size	5,141	5,930	5,193	5,492
Total Local Production	2,365	2,358	2,697	3,338
Total Exports	935	1,019	1,366	1,653
Total Imports	3,711	4,591	3,862	3,807

Source: Korea Aerospace Industries Association. Unit: USD Million.

Korea is the 10th largest market for U.S. aerospace exports. In 2012, total U.S. aerospace exports to Korea exceeded USD 3.4 billion (including aerospace products in the defense sector). In total value, U.S. aerospace sales constituted about 80% of Korea's total aerospace imports.

While imports are a significant portion of its high technology and aerospace products, over the last few years, Korea has continued to develop its capabilities to produce indigenous aerospace products, especially those requiring highly-advanced technologies. The country increasingly endeavors to emerge as an exporter of parts and components, as well as being a major industry player and supplier for some of the world's major manufacturers, including Boeing and Airbus. Korea's local production of aerospace products continues to grow, at USD 2.8 billion in 2012, while exports grew to USD 1.5 billion in 2012.

A 2010 Ministry of Knowledge Economy (MKE) report "*Aerospace Industry Primary Plan (2010 – 2019)*," explains a plan to raise Korea's aerospace production from USD 2 billion (2009) to USD 20 billion by 2020, raising exports to USD 10 billion, or 3 percent global market share. The industry plan aims to take Korea from 16th place to the world's seventh largest aerospace producer, within 10 years. Additionally, the parallel goal is to push Korean industry into importing core technologies, developing domestic capabilities to deliver a 'complete aircraft,' and bringing effective R&D investments which will further contribute to Korea's aerospace industry.

Korea's indigenous aerospace industry includes the production of military helicopters, super-sonic training jets (the "T-50" was the first supersonic jet developed in Korea, in conjunction with a U.S. defense company), UAVs, and MRO parts and components for both Boeing and EADS-Airbus.

In 2008, Korea Aerospace Industries (KAI) introduced its first non-military private aircraft, 'Naraon', making Korea the 28th nation in the world to build and fly an indigenous plane. Following that, in 2011, Korea Aerospace Research Institute (KARI) succeeded in developing an unmanned tilt-rotor aircraft with Korean Airlines (KAL), Korea's largest airline. If successful, Korea will be the first nation in the world, after the U.S., to commercialize a tilt rotor UAV. Additionally, in March 2013, KAI won a $1.22 billion contract to exclusively supply wing parts to Europe's Airbus SAS. The contract calls for the building of wing bottom panels (WBP) for Airbus' very popular A320 passenger jets.

This marks the single largest civilian aircraft components deal won by a local company in Korea.

On January 2013, Korea succeeded in launching a two-stage rocket, the Korea Space Launch Vehicle-1 (KSLV-1), from its Naro-Space Center on Korea's southwestern coast. Korea is only the 11th country in the world capable of sending a rocket and satellite into space.

Korea's aircraft parts and components industry is driven by Korean Airlines (KAL), which has one of the largest commercial fleets in Asia. KAL plays an important role in Korea's civil aerospace market. It has a total of 148 aircraft and is the largest consumer of aircraft, equipment, components and various aerospace services, as well as being one of the major exporters of aerospace parts and components.

Asiana Airlines is the second largest airline in Korea, currently operating a total of 80 aircraft. Additionally, there are five Low Cost Carriers (LCC): Jeju Air, Jin Air, Air Busan, Easta Air, and T-Way Air. All of these airlines have 'growth' in their forecasts.

In the first half of 2012, despite Korea's sluggish growth (2.3% GDP), over 22 million Koreans traveled outside Korea. This was twice the number compared with the first half of 2011. Some 1.5 million passengers utilized LCCs (over six percent of all Korean air travelers). This usage is expected to go to 10 percent in the near future.

Korea has two state-owned airport companies, Incheon International Airport Corporation (IIAC) and Korea Airport Corporation (KAC). IIAC is the nation's largest and has its main international airport in Incheon City. Incheon Airport was voted #1 in the 'airport service quality' survey for the eighth year in a row and has won the highest score in the Airport Service Quality (ASQ) category, organized by the Airports Council International (ACI), consisting of 1,700 airports around the world. It is also consistently named Best Airport in the Asia-Pacific and Best Airport in the 25 to 40 million passenger category.

KAC operates a total of 14 airports in Korea (Gimpo, Kimhae, Jeju, Daegu, Ulsan, Chunju, Muahn, Kwangju, Yeosu, Pohang, Yangyang, Sacheon, Kunsan, and Wonju), of which seven have international status, with routes mainly to either China or Japan.

Best Products/Services   Return to top

- Air Traffic Control Systems   - Avionics
- Radar   - Unmanned Aero Vehicle Systems

Opportunities   Return to top

Top U.S. aerospace exports to Korea include: complete aircraft, civilian aircraft engines, equipment and parts, military airplane parts, and helicopters. Korea is continuing to develop its indigenous aerospace industry, including the production of military helicopters, super-sonic jets, unmanned vehicles, MRO parts & components, and continued work-share for commercial aircraft components for Boeing and EADS-Airbus. The U.S. continues to be the dominant foreign supplier of aerospace/defense products and services, with a dominant import market share. This trend will continue for at least several years.

In April 2013, media sources disclosed the following growth plans for Korea's airlines:

- Korean Air will acquire nine new aircraft in 2013 and another 53 by 2018;
- Asiana Air will acquire four new aircraft in 2013; and
- The five LCCs have disclosed plans to acquire two new aircraft (each) in 2013.

Additionally, Korean Air and Boeing have recently announced a plan to build Asia's largest flight training center, to include a flight simulation center, in Incheon, Korea.

KORUS FTA Impact   Return to top

All of the U.S. aerospace exports are duty-free as of March 15, 2012, as a result of the implementation of the Korea-U.S. FTA (KORUS).

Resources   Return to top

Trade Shows
Korea Aerospace & Defense Exhibition (Seoul Air Show 2013)
Bi-annual: October 29 - November 3, 2013, KINTEX

Key Contacts
Korea Aerospace Industries Association (KAIA) – www.aerospace.or.kr
Korea Aerospace Research Institute (KARI) – www.kari.re.kr
Ministry of Trade, Industry and Energy – www.motie.go.kr/language/eng/index.jsp
Ministry of National Defense (MND) – www.mnd.go.kr

Local Contact
Ms. Sunny Park
Commercial Specialist
U.S. Commercial Service, Korea
U.S. Embassy Seoul
188 Sejong-daero, Jongro-gu
Seoul 110-710 Korea
Tel: 82-2-397-4164
E-mail: sunny.park@trade.gov
www.export.gov/southkorea

Cosmetics

ITA CODE: COS

Overview

Return to top

	2010	**2011**	**2012 (E)**
Total Market Size	5,457	5,947	6,538
Total Local Production	5,203	5,763	6,627
Total Exports	597	805	1,067
Total Imports	851	989	978
Imports from the U.S.	225	**257**	270

Exchange Rate: USD1= KW1,156 (2010), 1,108 (2011), 1,126 (2012);
Sources: Korea Pharmaceutical Traders Association (KPTA), Korea Cosmetic Association (KCA);
Unit: USD million.

Total imports of cosmetics in 2012 were estimated to be USD 978 million. Of these, U.S. imports were USD 270 million, representing an approximately 28 percent import market share. It is estimated that by 2013, the Korean cosmetics market will increase by approximately 10 percent over 2012 and reach a value of approximately USD 7 billion. The market is expected grow at an average annual rate of approximately 10-15 percent over the next several years.

According to industry sources, the growth of parallel imports and recently reduced tariff rates will contribute to increasing demand for quality foreign cosmetics. Also, the KORUS FTA will continue to eliminate Korean tariffs on imported U.S. cosmetics over a ten-year period. These market trends signal good opportunities for U.S. companies in the years ahead.

The Korean cosmetics market is polarized, with products focused both at the premium end and at the lower-priced, mass-market end. Thus, cosmetics companies focus their offerings towards two distinct groups of consumers or target audiences: consumers shopping at low-cost cosmetics franchise stores and those that are shopping for high-end luxury cosmetics, at more expensive department stores.

Sales of men's cosmetics have been and will continue expanding. This growth reflects the interest of Korean male consumers expanding from simple skincare to other cosmetics, such as facial scrubs, facial masks, concealers, SPF products, and other cosmeceutical products. With this trend, men's skincare salons have opened in business districts and now provide one-stop total beauty and hair care services, including hair cutting, perms, treatments, and facials. To meet this increasing demand for men's skincare products, many department stores have opened men's cosmetics counters on the men's floor, featuring recognized international brands like Clinique, Clarins and Biotherm, that offer after-shave lotions, cleaning foams, facial scrubs, facial packs, essences, and other functional cosmetics.

Best Prospects/Services

Return to top

- Natural/organic skincare products

- Functional cosmetics for both women and men
- Hair care cosmetics with special functions (e.g., to protect against hair loss)

Opportunities Return to top

Pharmacies and drug stores, catalogue sales, and newer channels such as on-line shopping malls and television home-shopping channels (such as QVC) have emerged as challengers to traditional retail channels like direct selling, multi-level marketing, "mom and pop" stores, specialty retail establishments, department stores, and discount stores.

There are currently three major franchise drug stores competing in the local market: Olive Young by CJ, W-Store by Kolon, and GS Watson's by GS (in partnership with Watson's). These retailers target customers focusing on wellness products by providing organic/natural cosmetics, nutritional supplements, OTC drugs, and general consumer goods. Furthermore, some major Korean cosmetics manufacturers are interested in importing well-known U.S. cosmetics.

Resources Return to top

Trade Shows
Seoul Cosmetics & Beauty Expo 2014
http://www.cosmobeautyseoul.com

Key Contacts
Korea Food & Drug Association (KFDA) - http://eng.kfda.go.kr/index.php
Korea Pharmaceutical Traders Association (KPTA) - http://www.kpta.or.kr/E_main.asp
Korea Cosmetic Association (KCA) - http://www.kcia.or.kr/eng/company/greeting.asp

Local Contact
Ms. Yoon-shil Chay
Senior Commercial Specialist
U.S. Embassy Seoul
188 Sejong-daero, Jongro-gu
Seoul 110-710 Korea
Tel: 82-2-397-4439
E-mail: Yoonshil.Chay@trade.gov

Defense Industry Equipment

ITA CODE: PR DFN

Overview Return to top

The Republic of Korea (ROK) has the world's sixth largest military force, following China, the U.S., India, North Korea, and Russia. South Korea's defense industry has grown far faster than the regional average in recent years, in order to counter the increasingly antagonistic actions of North Korea. The ROK continues to be a major defense and security ally of the U.S. in the Pacific region.

Continuing threats from North Korea, including the sinking of South Korea's navy vessel "Cheonan" (March 2010) and an artillery attack on South Korea's Yeonpyung Island (November 2010), plus the launch of a rocket in December of 2012 and a third nuclear explosion in February 2013, have prompted the ROK to allocate significant resources to develop its defense industry.

The ROK's defense industry is mainly focused on establishing an independent defense competence and modernizing infrastructure. The Ministry of National Defense (MND) has recently announced a continuation of their ambitious plan to optimize indigenous production, diversity suppliers, bolster air and space power, and procure sophisticated technology in the country's continual process of modernization and advancement.

In March 2011, the MND announced its revised "DRP 307" plan, designed to strengthen its defense against North Korea's localized military attacks and asymmetric threats, as well as to optimize a military command structure.

It is expected there will be a continued review on platform procurement requirements as Korea continues to revise what products/systems are needed, in light of a new threat assessment. It is also expected that the force improvement plan will focus more on command and control, land systems, maritime patrol/littoral support, and armor.

Market Demand

	2010	2011 (Estimated)	2012 (Projected)	2013 (Projected)
Total Market Size	8,275	8,812	8,994	9,180
Total Local Production	7,707	9,342	10,086	11,152
Total Exports	1,188	2,400	3,000	3,920
Total Imports	1,756	1,870	1,909	1,948
Imports from the U.S.	1,159	1,234	1,260	1,286
Exchange Rate: 1 USD	1,100	1,100	1,100	1,100

Note: The statistical data above is an unofficial estimate from CS Korea based on the budget of Korea's Force Improvement Plan (FIP), Defense Acquisition Program Administration (DAPA)'s procurement plan, and media reports. Unit: USD Million.

For 2013, a total of USD 30.66 billion has been allocated for Korea's defense budget, which includes USD 9.03 billion for the ROK's force improvement plan (FIP). The total budget and FIP budget received a 5.8 percent and a 2.2 percent increase, respectively, compared to the previous year.

Breakdown	2012	2013
Total Defense Budget	29,269	30,665
Force Improvement Plan (FIP)	8,787	9,032
Operation & Management (O&M)	20,482	21,633
Exchange Rate: 1 USD	1,126	1,120

USD millions

The FIP 2013 budget was increased to prepare for the increasing threat from North Korea and for the promotion and investment in local production capabilities and exports.

Korea has announced the following acquisition plans for several major defense projects:

- NF-III Next Generation Fighter (F-35 vs. F-155E): Acquisition of 60 aircraft worth USD 8 billion
- KF-X: Acquisition of 60 Next Generation Korean Fighters, worth USD 4.4 billion
- Air tanker/refueler: Acquisition of 4 refuelers, worth USD 6.5 billion
- Global Hawk: Acquisition of 4 HALE UAVs, worth USD 780 million
- AEW&C (E-737): Acquisition of 4 AWACs, worth USD 1.6 billion
- AH-X: Acquisition of 36 heavy attack helicopters, worth USD 2.5 billion
- KDX-III (AEGIS) Destroyer: Acquisition of 3 destroyers, worth USD 4 billion
- KSS-II Diesel Submarines: Acquisition of 9 submarines, worth USD 3 billion

Source: ROK Ministry of Strategy and Finance

With around 7.1% of the total budget allocated to defense R&D, the ROK is continually supporting local production capabilities, with great emphasis placed on exports, aiming for the total export of defense items from the ROK to reach USD 10 billion in five years.

In 2011, total exports of defense products were USD 2.4 billion, more than double 2010 levels (USD 1.1 billion) and 10 times higher than five years ago (USD 0.25 billion). This impressive growth is largely attributable to two major export contracts: T-50 trainer jet exports (16 units, USD 400 million) and submarine exports (3 units, USD 1.1 billion, Korea's biggest-ever defense export sale) -- both to Indonesia.

In recent bilateral meetings between the ROK and the U.S., the two countries have reaffirmed previous plans to transfer wartime military operational control to Seoul by December 2015. Wartime military operational control will be handed over to Korea's Joint Chiefs of Staff, from the Korea-U.S. Combined Forces Command.

Additionally, progress is being made regarding the relocation of the U.S. troops in Korea to Pyeongtaek, south of Seoul. The relocation comes under an agreement first reached in 2004, and then finalized in 2011, to relocate the American military bases in and around Seoul to Pyeongtaek, by the end of 2016. There are currently 28,500 U.S. troops stationed on more than 100 bases in Korea, stretching from the DMZ south to the port city of Busan. Plans call for consolidating the troops onto fewer than 50 bases, with the majority stationed in regional hubs in areas around Pyeongtaek/Osan and Daegu. The construction of housing, schools and medical and recreational facilities on bases south of Seoul has long been considered a key element in the U.S. plan to allow more troops to bring families to South Korea, allowing for longer tours and greater stability among the ranks on the Korean peninsula.

Market Access & Obstacles

The ROK's defense procurement agency, the Defense Acquisition Program Administration (DAPA), is the sole government agency conducting and executing the procurement of defense equipment. Established in 2006, DAPA is the only agency authorized to negotiate on behalf of the Ministry of National Defense (MND) for defense products and services, as well as being the only agency that can authorize offset credits, dictate terms and conditions, and make changes to delivery schedules or required deliverables. DAPA controls all formal negotiations on price, technology transfer, local work share, and offset packages, which are required by the Korean government for all projects in excess of USD 10 million. A large portion of Korea's export of defense products is a result of DAPA's defense offset program.

In 2010, DAPA announced new guidelines on the utilization of commissioned agents. The new policy requires DAPA to enter into contract directly with foreign prime contractors, without the intervention of a commissioned agent for major acquisition programs (those exceeding USD 2 million). The policy applies only to Force Improvement Programs (FIP), which includes purchases, development, upgrades, and associated installations. Smaller value FIP projects and sustainment projects are not affected.

U.S. Position in Korea's Defense Industry

The U.S. remains Korea's most significant military ally, owing largely to the presence of 28,500 U.S. troops in Korea as a deterrent to aggression from North Korea. This has historically affected defense procurement decisions. The U.S. continues to be a primary supplier in Korea, but the presence of other major suppliers (like Germany and Israel) is increasing. Recently (January 2013), Korea selected AugustaWestland, a Finmeccanica company, over U.S. companies, to supply AW159 helicopters to meet its maritime operational helicopter requirement. With increasing competition from European competitors, U.S. companies still maintain a significant position in the Korean defense market and are expected to do so into the future.

The U.S. provided weapons systems to South Korea totaling USD 1,159 million in 2010, which accounted for 66 percent of Korea's total defense imports. U.S. standards are generally accepted in Korea and most Korean defense systems are based upon American standards.

Direct commercial sales in the defense industry account for 54 percent of DAPA procurement (an average figure, from 2004 to 2011), but the MND encourages more government-to-government (FMS - Foreign Military Sales) programs, in an effort to reduce costs.

End-users

The principal point of contact for major defense projects are the service branches (ROKAF, ROKA, ROKN) and DAPA (Defense Acquisition Program Administration). These branches procure all necessary equipment and systems through DAPA. For projects requiring local co-production or co-development, foreign firms very often participate in consortia with leading local firms such as KAI, Hyundai Heavy Industries (HHI), and Samsung Thales, etc.

Sub-Sector Best Prospects Return to top

- C4ISR
- Military aerospace (fighters, multi-role airlift aircraft)
- Avionics
- Maritime defense electronics and systems

Opportunities Return to top

- Aircraft upgrades (fighters, multi-role airlift aircraft)
- Asymmetric warfare/littoral/coastal surveillance and patrol
- Support for combat equipment, including fighter aircraft

Web Resources Return to top

Trade Shows

Seoul International Aerospace & Defense Exhibition 2013 (Seoul Air Show 2013), October 29 to November 3, 2013 (http://www.seoulairshow.com). Please contact Kallman Worldwide, Inc. (http://www.kallman.com/), the official U.S. Pavilion organizers for ADEX 2013, for the U.S. Dept. of Commerce.

Naval & Defense 2013
October 22-25, 2013 - http://www.marineweek.org/naval_defence/main.php?lang=EN

As the Defense Acquisition Program Agency (DAPA) conducts formal contracting in South Korea, presentations to DAPA can be effective marketing tools to introduce new products/systems/services. DAPA provides this opportunity every two or three months. Consult: http://www.dapa.go.kr to confirm future scheduling.

Local Contact

Ms. Sunny Park
Commercial Specialist
U.S. Commercial Service, Korea
U.S. Embassy Seoul
188 Sejong-daero, Jongno-gu
Seoul 110-710 Korea
Tel: 82-2-397-4164
E-mail: sunny.park@trade.gov
http://www.export.gov/southkorea

Education Services

ITA CODE: SV EDS

Overview   Return to top

	2011	2012 (estimated)	2013 (estimated)	2014 (estimated)
Total Market Size	42,946	42,409	42,500	42,650
Total Local Production	38,476	38,361	38,330	38,442
Total Exports	55	70	85	97
Total Imports	4,525	4,118	4,255	4,305
Imports from the U.S.	1,129	1,030	1,132	1,142
Exchange Rate: 1 USD	1,108	1,126	1,126	1,126

Sources: Bank of Korea, Ministry of Education, Science & Technology, and Statistics Korea. Note: Total Market Size = Total Local Production + Total Imports – Total Exports. Total Local Production=Total educational expenditures by Korean families. Total Exports=Total educational expenditures of foreign students in Korea. Total Imports =Total educational expenditures of Korean students studying abroad. Imports from U.S = Total educational expenditure of Korean students studying in the U.S. Unit: USD millions.

In Korea, education, from pre-kindergarten to college, is 'king.' It plays a very significant role in the Korean economy and is part of the Korean psyche. There are good opportunities for a wide swath of U.S. educational institutions, if they are prepared to meet a highly sophisticated, demanding and brand-oriented marketplace. According to the Organization for Economic Cooperation and Development (OECD), Korea is one of the largest investors in education among all developed countries.

Higher education is synonymous with privilege and power in Korea. A degree from a well-known institution is a status symbol and essential for finding the 'right job in the right company.' Coveted spaces in Korea's top schools are open to competition from all students, but attainable for only a few. Many talented students instead opt for the best schools outside the country and obtain a diploma from an accredited overseas school. This translates into opportunities for U.S. schools to recruit some of Korea's most talented students. Koreans remain willing to spend a substantial portion of their income on education.

According to the Student and Exchange Visitor Information System (SEVIS), a total of 98,471 Korean students are enrolled in U.S. institutions (2013). Korea, with a population of 50 million, has ranked second behind China (with a population close to a billion), followed by India, in terms of the number of foreign students studying in the U.S. over the last few years. Some 289,288 students are studying abroad, per the Korean Ministry of Education. Korean students are generally going to the following markets: the U.S., 25 percent; China, 22 percent; Australia, 12 percent; Japan, 9 percent; the UK, 6 percent; Canada, 5 percent; other countries, 21 percent.

Korea recorded one of the lowest birthrates in the world, with around 1.2 children per family in 2012 (OECD). While the overall number of Koreans going abroad peaked in 2011, it decreased by 9% in 2012, for the first time in four years. Despite the decline of Korea's young population, Korea will likely continue as one of the top sources of international students who have the financial resources to travel abroad. As well, these students will uniformly achieve high academic performance at the U.S. institutions they attend.

The reputation of an educational institution has been key for students seeking a degree in higher education, whereas students studying in short-term programs (including university-to-university programs) focus on things like cost, living conditions, and also reputation. Since the global financial crisis of 2008 to Korea's present sluggish economy, the trend has been that Korean families are increasingly employing strategies to lower the cost of education. One way is by studying at a community college before transferring to a four-year school, or studying English in a low-cost country before applying to an American school.

Sub-Sector Best Prospects Return to top

• One-year exchange programs for elementary and secondary school students
• Community colleges
• One- or two-semester exchange programs for college students

Opportunities Return to top

Recently, a growing number of Korean students began taking advantage of exchange programs or 'one-way' programs (i.e., Korean students pay the tuition to U.S. institutions that combine English language and credit courses). Korean students also express a high interest in programs that incorporate other value-added components, such as internships or training in job interview techniques.

Korean parents are now savvier about acquiring information on educational opportunities for their children. Agents or reps are utilized less often. Educational entities should consider employing a combination of on-line advertising, blogging, personally visiting middle and high schools, alumni groups, social media, advertisements via popular search engines, Korean-American newspapers in the U.S., and advertising in business newspapers and/or on cable TV/radio in Korea. Koreans prefer educational entities that have a long-term commitment to Korea and its students.

Web Resources Return to top

Trade Shows

Korea Study Abroad & Emigration Fair - http://www.yuhak2min.com/new_www/intro.html

MBA Tours - http://www.thembatour.com/index.shtml

University Fair (organized by Linden Tours) - http://www.lindentours.com

Korea Student Fair - http://www.aief-usa.org/

Key Contacts

Ministry of Education - http://english.moe.go.kr/enMain.do

Fulbright (Korean-American Educational Commission) -
http://www.fulbright.or.kr/xe/?mid=index_en

KOSA (Korea Overseas Studying Agencies) - http://www.kosaworld.org/

Local Contact

Ms. Young Hee Koo
Commercial Specialist
U.S. Commercial Service, Korea
U.S. Embassy Seoul
188 Sejong-daero, Jongno-gu
Seoul 110-710 Korea
Tel: 82-2-397-4396
E-mail: younghee.koo@trade.gov
http://www.export.gov/southkorea

Energy: New and Renewable (NRE)

ITA CODE: PR REQ

Overview   Return to top

	2010	2011	2012 (estimated)	2013 (estimated)
Total Market Size	4,002	7,289	8,205	8,285
Total Local Production	6,988	13,481	17,391	17,538
Total Exports	4,532	7,650	10,700	10,486
Total Imports	1,547	1,458	1514	1530
Imports from the U.S.	NA	NA	NA	NA
Korean government investment plan	466	622	588	617
Exchange Rate: 1 USD	1,156	1,108	1,126.00	1,120.00

Total Market Size = (Total Local Production + Total Imports – Total Exports);
Data Sources: Korea Energy Management Corporation (KEMCO); Korea Energy Management Corporation (KEMCO) and Ministry of Knowledge Economy (MKE); Imports from U.S.: NA; Unit: USD million.

According to the Korea Energy Management Corporation (KEMC), Korea's energy consumption has increased sharply since the mid-1970s, due primarily to the rapid economic growth propelled by the heavy and chemical industries. Total primary energy consumption, which stood at 43.9 million tons of oil equivalent (TOE) in 1980, increased more than six-fold, to 275.7 million TOE in 2011, ranking Korea as the 10th largest energy consuming nation in the world. Energy consumption per capita also increased rapidly, from 1.1 TOE in 1980 to 5.1 TOE in 2011.

As of the end of 2011, NRE supply totaled 7,583 thousand TOE and comprised 2.75 percent of total primary energy consumption. Of the total supply of NRE, waste energy contributed the largest proportion, with 67.54 percent, following by hydro power, with 12.73 percent, and other types of energy, such as photovoltaic (PV), with 19.73 percent. KEMC estimates that the NRE share of primary energy supply will account for 4.3% in 2015, 6.1% in 2020, and 11.0% in 2030.

NRE power generation has increased rapidly, in particular in the PV and wind areas, thanks to the introduction of the FIT (Feed in Tariff) and RPS (Renewable Portfolio Standard) systems. In terms of PV, power generation has increased nearly 30 times, to 917,198 MWh in 2011, from 31,022 MWh in 2006; Wind increased to 862,884 MWh from 238,911 MWh. Fuel cells appeared as an electricity source in 2006; as of 2010, their output was almost 44 times higher, at 294,621 MWh. NRE generation accounted for 17,345 GWh (1.24%) of the total 501,527,009 GWh of electricity generated in 2011 (waste power generation accounted for 58.8%).

In the Korean government's 3rd national NRE basic plan, waste and hydro are projected to decrease, while marine energy, geothermal, solar thermal and wind energy are expected to increase. The bio-energy share will grow to 31.4% and take the second largest position, just behind waste energy.

Sub-Sector Best Prospects   Return to top

Photovoltaic power: Next-generation solar cells, including thin-film modules and roof-top systems, are expected to generate substantial demand in the future.

Wind power: With oceans on three sides, Korea's focus on wind-power is rapidly shifting from ground applications to offshore applications.

Fuel cells: Korea is home to some of the world's largest hydrogen & fuel cell power plants. With ROKG's strong policy support and Korean industry's active participation, the fuel cell industry is forecast to grow to be one of the most rapidly growing NRE sectors in the future.

Marine energy: Korea has abundant access to marine energy and is aggressively emphasizing such developments through on-going R&D projects and pilot construction projects.

Integrated gasification and combined cycle (IGCC): Due to the high efficiency and environmental feature of this technology, Korea has plans to adopt it for new coal-fired plants, including one with a capacity of 300 MW currently planned to be completed by 2013 (project of the Korea Western Power Company).

Opportunities   Return to top

The Korea Electric Power Corporation (KEPCO) is the government-run power company and the primary end-user of NRE products and services. It supplies more than 90 percent of Korea's entire electricity needs from its six generating subsidiaries (Gencos) that include five fossil fuel-fired companies and one nuclear-hydro company. Required by the ROK's NRE policy initiatives, the Gencos have diversified their energy sources and are now generating a stable amount of electricity from low-carbon methods. There will be a need to continue to shift the power source to NRE, since RPS will be fully in effect by 2013.

The six Gencos are:

- Korea Hydro and Nuclear Company (KHNP): http://www.khnp.co.kr/index_en.jsp
- Korea South-East Power Company, Ltd. (KOSEP): www.kosep.co.kr
- Korea Midland Power Company, Ltd. (KOMIPO): http://www.komipo.co.kr/
- Korea Western Power Company, Ltd. (KOWEPO): http://www.westernpower.co.kr
- Korea Southern Power Company, Ltd. (KOSPO): http://www.kospo.co.kr
- Korea East-West Power Company, Ltd. (KEWESPO): http://www.kewp.com

As end-users, the Gencos and the fledgling independent power producers (IPPs) exert strong influence in choosing what NRE core parts to use. Under the current supply chain, engineering & construction companies (E&Cs) which provide turn-key construction services are typically the buyers of most NRE technologies and parts. There are several large EPC companies, which are mostly subsidiaries of Korea's business conglomerates (Samsung, Hyundai, SK, GS, etcetera). Many NRE power plant construction projects are led by business consortia that consist of end-users, EPC companies, financial service entities, and equity investors. These consortia collectively influence major procurement decisions.

Web Resources   Return to top

Trade Shows

Solar Con Korea - Feb.12-14, 2014/COEX, Seoul, Korea-
http://www.semiconkorea.org/en/

Expo Solar/PV Korea – September 4-6, 2013/KINTEX, Ilsan
http://www.exposolar.org/2013/

International Green Energy Expo Korea 2014, April 2014 (TBD), EXCO, Daegu -
http://www.energyexpo.co.kr/eng/

Solar Wind Earth Energy Trade Show (SWEET), 2014 (TBD), KDJ Center -
http://www.sweet.or.kr/eng/index.php

Korea Energy Show - October 16-19, 2013/COEX -
http://www.koreaenergyshow.or.kr/ab-2966015-2&tpa_index192=10

Key Contacts
Korea Energy Management Corp. (KEMCO) - www.kemco.or.kr/new_eng/main/main.asp
Ministry of Trade, Industry and Energy – www.motie.go.kr/language/eng/index.jsp
Korea Customs Service (KCS) - http://english.customs.go.kr

Local Contact
Ms. Alex Choi
Commercial Specialist
U.S. Commercial Service Korea
U.S. Embassy Seoul
188, Sejong-daero, Chongno-gu
Seoul 110-710 Korea
Tel: 82-2-397-4466
E-mail: Alex.Choi@trade.gov
http://www.export.gov/southkorea

Entertainment and Media

ITA CODE: N/A

Overview Return to top

	2011	2012	2013 (E)	2014 (E)
Total Market Size	2,542.06	2,663.34	2,775.95	2,940.37
Total Local Production	3,910.86	4,097.44	4,270.70	4,697.77
Total Exports	1,955.43	2,097.44	2,135.35	2,391.59
Total Imports	586.63	614.62	640.60	634.19
Imports from the U.S.	234.65	245.62	256.24	258.50
Exchange Rate: USD1	1,108	1,126	1,120	1,100

Source: Korea Creative Content Agency (KOCCA), Korea Film Council (KOFIC); Unit: USD million.

Films

Market Share of Films by Country

	Korea	U.S.	China	Europe	Japan	Others
2012	57.6	35.7	0.3	4.8	1.2	0.4
2011	48.9	46.7	0.3	1.8	1.6	0.7

Source: Korea Film Council (KOFIC); Unit = %

In 2012, the Korean film industry had some of the best revenues and profitability results in recent memory.

The total number of filmgoers in 2012 was over 114 million, an increase of 21.9 percent from 2011. The market share of Korean films increased to 57.6 percent, from 48.9 percent in 2011. In 2012, 229 Korean films were produced, though only 175 films were released. Likewise, 773 foreign films were imported and rated, an increase of 40% over 2011, and 456 were released. Although the number of screens is limited to a little over 2,000 per year, imported content is increasing, due to competition among the various platforms and the fact that locally-produced content insufficient to cover the needs of all platforms.

Number of Korean Films Produced, Foreign Content Imported, and Total Films Released

	Korean Films		Foreign Films		Total films released
	# of films produced	# of films released	# of films imported	# of films released	
2010	152	140	383	286	426
2011	216	150	551	289	439
2012	229	175	773	456	631

Opportunities Return to top

Growth of Digital On-Line Market

The consumption of content in Korea is increasingly via on-line services, utilizing both wired and wireless communications. Through various on-line services such as IPTV, Video-on-Demand/VOD (downloading and streaming) and mobile services, the digital content market is growing rapidly. In 2012, demand for digital on-line services, which has shown more than 20% growth for three consecutive years, was over USD 200 million. This rapid growth is led by IPTV and digital cable TV.

As of 2012, the number of IPTV subscribers was 6.4 million, with digital cable TV subscribers at just over 5 million. More than 11 million households have the capability to watch digital content and each household may have multiple members accessing different types of content. The growth of digital subscribers also resulted in increases in on-line services utilizing content. Sixty-one percent of market demand for digital on-line services is for IPTV and digital cable TV.

The growth of on-line services has led to a change in one of TV's main characteristics. In the past, TV provided programmed broadcasts to viewers, who had no choice in what they could watch at a particular time on any one channel. Today, viewers can choose any program at any time. This change in the environment has resulted in increasing competition among platforms. Thus, they need more content than ever. TV is the most competitive platform as far as consumption of content by individuals, as the utilization rate of TV is approximately 98 percent.

Broadcasting Content

According to a survey conducted by the Korea Creative Content Agency (KOCCA), the import of broadcasting content has increased by 6.2 percent over 2010. The import of cable TV content increased by 8.0 percent over 2010, while that of terrestrial TV content actually decreased. Terrestrial TV imported US$ 3.7 million worth of content, representing 3.4 percent of total content imports. Cable TV recorded US$153 million in imports, which was 96 percent of total imports. Independent production companies imported US$654,000, or 0.6 percent of imports.

By genre, 55.4 percent (US$57.5 million) of total imports were films, followed by television dramas at 38.1 percent (US$ 40 million). Documentary imports were recorded at 3.6 percent of total imports (US$ 3.7 million). For terrestrial TV, documentaries were 63.7 percent of total imports, followed by films (16.1 percent), animation (11.4 percent), and drama (8.6 percent). For cable TV and the independent production companies, 56.7 percent of total imports were films, followed by dramas (39.1 percent), entertainment programs (2.2 percent), and documentaries (1.6 percent).

By country, North America, including the U.S., has an overwhelmingly high share of imported broadcasting content, at 94.4 percent, followed by the UK, at 1.7 percent, and Europe and Japan, each with a share of 1.2 percent.

Web Resources Return to top

Trade Shows

Busan Int'l Film Festival:	http://www.biff.kr
KCTA Show:	http://www.kctashow.com/eng/main.html
Busan Contents Market:	http://www.ibcm.tv/eng/index.php
Asian Film Market:	http://www.asianfilmmarket.org/structure/eng/default.asp

Key Contacts

Korea Communications Commission:	http://eng.kcc.go.kr/user/ehpMain.do
Ministry of Culture, Sports and Tourism:	http://www.mcst.go.kr/english/index.jsp
Korea Creative Content Agency:	http://www.kocca.kr/eng/index.html
Korea Cable TV Association:	www.kcta.or.kr (Only Korean available)
Korea Film Council:	http://www.koreanfilm.or.kr/jsp/index.jsp

Local Contact
Ms. Alex Choi
Commercial Specialist
U.S. Commercial Service, Korea
U.S. Embassy Seoul
188, Sejong-daero, Chongno-gu
Seoul 110-710 Korea
Tel: 82-2-397-4466
E-mail: Alex.choi@trade.gov
http://www.export.gov/southkorea

Franchising

ITA CODE: SV FRA

Overview Return to top

Franchising in Korea is a USD 84.3 billion (2012) industry, with potential to grow in a wide array of service and new food sectors. Koreans are avid and demanding consumers.

Nearly 3,034 franchises were registered in Korea in 2011. According to the 2012 Yearbook of Retail Industries, some 21,121 convenience store franchises are operating in Korea, of which 5,085 opened in 2011. Nearly 2,145 were food service franchises, 276 were retail franchises, and 613 were service franchises. On average, a master franchise operates 68.5 stores across its industry in Korea.

Over the past few years, CS Korea has discovered that the Korean franchise market is heavily concentrated with food service and other retail franchise operations. In fact, the number of food service franchises (1,962) was three times bigger than that of non-food service franchises (593) registered in Korea in 2011. This is differentiated by the situation in the United States and other economically-advanced countries, where non-food service franchises account for an exceptionally large part of the total market. Franchise experts in Korea note that future U.S. investors should try tapping into the non-food service franchise segments.

Franchising Market Sales in Korea – 2011

Industry Sector	Sales
Food Service	USD 7.8 (22.4%)
Service	USD 6.6 (19.0%)
Retail	USD 20.4 (58.6%)
Total	USD 34.8 (100%)

Sources: Korea's Franchising Industry - 2011 by Korea Chamber of Commerce & Industry Retail db (KCCI).

Franchisors interested in this market must:

- Meet the rules promulgated under Korea's Fair Transactions in Franchise Business Act
- Be registered with the Korea Fair Trade Commission
- Comply with the sub-franchisee's Fair Trade Act requirements, which stipulate the need for disclosure of all business information to potential sub-franchisees, at least 14 days before signing an agreement. This Act closely parallels the rules that exist for sub-franchisees in the U.S.

Since the 1980s, all the major first-, second- and third-tier U.S. food chain franchises have either (1) been successful in Korea, (2) have been here and failed, or (3) are trying to return -- a very difficult proposition in a country that doesn't forget a failed enterprise. Interested parties should consult our 2012 Industry Sector Analysis (ISA) report on franchising (available upon request).

The March 2013 entry into force of the KORUS FTA is positively affecting this industry in many ways, including:

- Expedited Customs Procedures: Improved transparency through the publication of Customs measures ensures that U.S. companies have access to Customs laws and regulations. In addition, KORUS requires simplified Customs procedures, for the timely and efficient release of goods.

- Protected U.S. Investment: A stable legal framework protects all forms of U.S. investment. With few exceptions, U.S. investors will be treated just like Korean investors in the establishment, acquisition and operation of investments in Korea.

As part of Korea's efforts in 2012 and 2013 to bring about 'economic democratization,' the National Commission for Corporate Partnership (NCCP) recommended that regulations be imposed on large companies/conglomerates, to provide opportunities and raise the competitiveness of SMEs in the franchise sector. The NCCP classifies large companies/conglomerates and those with annual sales of over 20 billion Korean won with more than 200 employees under the Minor Enterprise Basic Law. A whole series of restrictions, such as denying a conglomerate the ability to open a new store located less than 500 meters from an existing shop of the same brand, is expected to go into force in 2013. At present, there are no exceptions for foreign companies operating in Korea, if their annual sales are over 20 billion won and with more than 200 employees.

The NCCP's new regulations will be in effect for approximately three years, from approximately mid-2013 to mid-2016. Franchise brands must follow these rules or will be penalized with fines imposed by Korea's Small and Medium Business Administration (KSMBA). At this writing, with regulations still in draft form, it is assumed that about 30 companies (chaebols) will be affected by these regulations or 'semi-official rules.' Chaebols are already proving unwilling to 'rock-the-boat' in reference to these regulations.

While the effects of economic democratization and the NCCP's new regulations will likely have a dampening effect on U.S. franchisors, opportunities do exist in Korea's nearly half-dozen new cities or communities that are growing and gaining momentum.

Resources   Return to top

Trade Shows
The 29th Korea Franchise Business Expo 2013
http://www.kfaexpo.kr (English website is not available)

Franchise Seoul 2013 (Spring)
http://franchiseseoul.co.kr (English website is not available)

Franchise Seoul 2013 (Fall)
http://franchisechangup.co.kr (English website is not available)

Key Contacts
Korea Franchise Association (KFA) - http://www.ikfa.org
National Commission for Corporate Partnership (NCCP) - http://www.winwingrowth.or.kr
Korea Chamber of Commerce & Industry (KCCI) - http://english.korcham.net

Korea Fair Trade Commission (KFTC) - http://eng.ftc.go.kr

Local Contact
Ms. Grace Sung
Commercial Specialist
U.S. Commercial Service, Korea
U.S. Embassy Seoul
188 Sejong-daero, Jongro-gu
Seoul 110-710 Korea
Tel: 82-2-397-4324
E-mail: Grace.Sung@trade.gov
(Interim contact until Fall 2013: Ms. Yujin Jo - yujin.jo@trade.gov)

Laboratory Scientific Instruments

ITA CODE: PR LAB

Overview Return to top

	2011	2012 (estimated)	2013 (estimated)	2014 (estimated)
Total Market Size	2,992	3,520	3,942	4,336
Total Local Production	1,283	1,510	1,691	1,860
Total Exports	136	160	179	197
Total Imports	1,845	2,170	2,430	2,673
Imports from the U.S.	553	651	729	802
Exchange Rate: 1 USD	1,108	1,126	1,126	1,126

Source: Korea International Trade Association (KITA) & National Research Facilities & Equipment Center.
Unit: USD millions.

Korea's market demand for laboratory scientific instruments was estimated at US$ 3.5 billion in 2012, an 8% increase from the previous year. Korea depends heavily on imports in this sector and over 62% of total market demand is met by foreign suppliers. U.S. companies are leading suppliers, with a 30% share of the market, followed closely by Japan with 26% and Germany with 23%. The U.S. dominates the upper-end, high value-added segment of the market.

For the last five years, Korea's R&D budgets have recorded an annual increase of 15%, with a 10-12% increase expected over the next five years, reaching $58 billion by 2014. Investment in laboratory scientific instruments alone takes up an average of 8% of Korea's total annual R&D expenditures. The healthy increase of R&D budgets is expected to generate steady demand for laboratory scientific instruments.

The largest end-users of laboratory scientific instruments over the past six years were the 25 government-funded research institutes. These institutes consumed 36% of all of Korea's total investment in scientific instruments.

Universities ranked second, with 19%. Private enterprises took a 13% share, including the electronics, automotive, chemicals, materials, and pharmaceutical sectors. The main private buyers included private research labs affiliated with major Korean conglomerates, including Samsung, LG, SK and Hyundai, as well as independent pharmaceutical/biotechnology companies.

Sub-Sector Best Prospects Return to top

The following six industrial and technological areas have the best sales potential:

- Environment
- Biotechnology
- Nanotechnology
- Information technology
- Semiconductors

- Computers

Opportunities   Return to top

Technology development related to Korea's New Growth Engine segments will continue to provide lucrative opportunities for laboratory scientific instruments and include:

- Green technology industries, i.e., water treatment, green transportation systems, IT convergence, and LEDs, to name a few
- High-tech convergence, to include broadcast and communications media, intelligent robots, biopharmaceutical and medical devices, IT, food industry, and nano-convergence.

Web Resources   Return to top

Trade Shows
The 10th Int'l R&D · Analysis Equipment Exhibition 2013 (AnaLab 2013), Korea (http://analab.or.kr/)
The 7th KOREA LAB 2013, Korea (http://eng.korealab.org/)

Key Contacts
National Research Facilities & Equipment Center -
http://www.nfec.go.kr/html/kr/index.html
National Science and Technology Commission - http://www.pps.go.kr/english/

Local Contact
Ms. Young Hee Koo
Commercial Specialist
U.S. Commercial Service, Korea
U.S. Embassy Seoul
188 Sejong-daero, Jongno-gu
Seoul 110-710 Korea
Tel: 82-2-397-4396
E-mail: younghee.koo@trade.gov
http://www.export.gov/southkorea

Medical Equipment and Devices

ITA CODE: PR MED

Overview
Return to top

Unit: USD thousands

	2011	2012 (estimated)	2013 (estimated)	2014 (estimated)
Total Market Size	3,886,000	4,313,000	4,744,000	5,219,000
Total Local Production	3,038,000	3,372,000	3,709,000	4,080,000
Total Exports	1,673,000	1,857,000	2,043,000	2,247,000
Total Imports	2,521,000	2,798,000	3,078,000	3,386,000
Imports from the U.S.	1,119,000	1,253,000	1,378,000	1,516,000
Exchange Rate: 1 USD	1,108	1,126	1,126	1,126

Total Market Size = (Total Local Production + Total Imports) – (Total Exports)
Source: Korea Medical Devices Industry Association, KMDIA

The Korean medical device market is estimated to reach USD 4.9 billion in 2013. One factor that may slow import growth will be pricing and reimbursement measures the Korean government grapples with under its national healthcare system.

Korea depends on high-end medical devices, as listed below, from the U.S., EU, and Japan, to supply about 65 percent of total market demand. Korean companies make comparatively lower-end (mid-technology) medical devices. Another factor favoring the use of imported advanced medical equipment and devices is the growing elderly population, as well as Korean doctors educated in the U.S. and Europe, who are accustomed to using advanced medical devices.

In 2011, total imports of medical devices were USD 2.5 billion, with U.S. imports totaling over USD 1.1 billion. The U.S. market share represents 44 percent of the import market. Market demand for foreign advanced and innovative medical devices is estimated to have experienced slow growth in 2012. The Korean economy has not fully recovered to its pre-global financial crisis levels.

The importation of medical devices requires the assignment of an importer or representative based in Korea to manage medical device approvals and to ensure regulatory compliance. As part of pre-market approval requirements, the Government of Korea requires testing reports of imported devices for safety and efficacy. In addition to medical device approvals, companies also need to negotiate pricing terms with the Korean Health Insurance Review & Assessment Service (HIRA) and the National Health Insurance Corporation (NHIC).

Current issues for the medical device industry in Korea include reimbursement pricing and the healthcare technology assessment system for medical devices. The U.S. Embassy in Korea works closely with associations, including AdvaMed and the American Chamber of Commerce in Korea, to ensure that U.S. interests are well represented in the medical device industry.

The KORUS FTA was implemented on March 15, 2012. U.S. medical device and pharmaceutical companies now have the ability to voice their objections to pricing and maximum reimbursement conditions, imposed on U.S. products through the *Independent Review Process*. Established to regulate medical devices and drug prices, this review process is independent of the Ministry of Health and Welfare (MHW), the National Health Insurance Corporation (NHIC), and the Health Insurance Review and Assessment Service (HIRAS).

Sub-Sector Best Prospects Return to top

- Stents
- CT systems
- MRI systems
- Knee implants
- Soft contact lenses
- Kidney dialysis devices
- Catheters
- Lenses for eye glasses
- Ultrasound imaging systems
- Intraocular lenses

Opportunities Return to top

A potential area for U.S.-Korea cooperation in the healthcare technology sector is in the area of clinical trials. Korea is interested in developing a more robust clinical trial environment for medical devices and pharmaceuticals. To attract foreign clinical trials to Korea, the Korean government will support and enhance the quality of relevant medical industries, such as globally-certified hospitals and high-end medical technologies, to be able to participate in clinical trials more frequently. U.S. companies that need clinical trials for their medical devices may contact the Director of Clinical Trials/Management Division, through their Korean importer, at ctmt@korea.kr, for details.

Web Resources Return to top

Trade Shows
Korea International Medical, Clinical, Laboratories & Hospital Equipment Show 2014
www.kimes.co.kr

Key Contacts
Ministry of Health and Welfare (MHW) – www.mw.go.kr
Ministry of Food and Drug Safety – www.mfds.go.kr
Health Insurance Review & Assessment Service (HIRA) - www.hira.or.kr

Local Contact
Ms. Yoon-Shil Chay
Senior Commercial Specialist
U.S. Commercial Service, Korea
U.S. Embassy Seoul
188 Sejong-daero, Jongno-gu
Seoul 110-710 Korea

Tel: 82-2-397-4439
E-mail: yoonshil.chay@trade.gov
http://www.export.gov/southkorea

Pollution Control Equipment

ITA CODE: PR POL

Overview

Unit: Million USD

	2007	2008	2009	2010	2011 (est.)	2012 (est.)	2013 (Projected)
Total Market Size	5,609	4,510	5,075	6,979	8,032	8,534	9,338
Total Local Production	6,166	5,421	5,642	7,858	9,018	9,759	10,795
Total Exports	1,135	1,539	1,250	1,621	1,787	2,088	2,388
Total Imports	578	628	683	742	800	863	931
Imports from the U.S.	173	188	205	223	240	259	279
Exchange Rate: 1 USD	929	1,105	1,276	1,156	1,108	1,126	1,120

Note: The above statistics are unofficial estimates by Commercial Service Korea, based on information published by the Ministry of Environment and industry experts.

Since Korea's implementation of its Low Carbon, Green Growth Strategy in 2009, the country continues to demonstrate a strong commitment to environmental improvement. The pollution control equipment industry continues to grow in various areas, such as water treatment, power plants and steel mills, with support from the government. Korea established a national-level industry technology road map, called "Eco-TRM 2022," in 2012, and began to embrace the development and dissemination of environmental technologies under the Support for Environmental Technology and Environment Industry Act of 2011.

CS Korea estimates the size of the pollution control equipment industry at USD 8.5 billion in 2012. According to industry experts, imports account for about 10 percent of the total market. Japan has been the principal foreign suppler, with about a 50 percent import market share, followed by the U.S. with about 30 percent market share, followed by Germany and France.

Local environmental equipment manufacturers in Korea have supplied a major portion of environmental projects with medium-level technology and moderate cost products. While they have significantly improved technical levels, mostly via technology transfers and mergers with non-Korean suppliers, local manufacturers still lack core technologies to supply products that meet the government's stringent regulatory requirements. They are therefore seeking more advanced imported products and technologies. Because most competing Korean manufacturers target larger volumes and export markets, highly customized solutions for specific applications, like in-house recycling and ultra-pure water treatment, offer potential for U.S. exporters.

Sub-Sector Best Prospects

- Carbon capture & storage technologies and equipment

- Volatile organic compounds (VOCs) control in oil refineries and petrochemical plants
- Dioxin abatement in municipal and industrial incinerators
- Advanced sulfur oxides/nitrogen oxides abatement in power plants and steel mills
- Energy saving and waste-to-energy in steel mills and municipal landfills
- Pollution-free and low-emission vehicles in engineering technology, engine components and parts for CNG
- Pollution abatement technologies for the automobile and oil refinery industries
- Advanced water pollution control technologies
- Environmentally-friendly construction materials

Opportunities   Return to top

The Korean government plays a key role in the pollution control equipment industry, serving as both the regulator and the largest end-user in this area. The 2013 national expenditure for environmental protection increased by approximately 5.3 percent from the previous year and is set at USD 5.49 billion.

Korean government project tenders are announced on the Korean government procurement (PPS) website, with detailed information on project scope and contact information (http://www.pps.go.kr/english/). For more information on PPS, readers are encouraged to review the "Selling to the Government" section of chapter three of this guide.

To enter the pollution control equipment market, we recommend that U.S. suppliers partner with qualified and capable Korean companies, which maintain existing sales networks to serve end-users and which are fully aware of the regulatory changes that drive the market. Exhibiting at local environmental trade shows can also be a good platform to explore the market, as well as gain exposure to end-users.

Web Resources   Return to top

Trade Shows
International Exhibition on Environmental Technologies (ENVEX 2013) -
http://www.envex.or.kr/english/main/main.asp
Water Korea 2012 - http://www.wakoex.co.kr/main/index.asp

Key Contacts
Ministry of Environment - http://eng.me.go.kr/main.do
Korea National Cleaner Production Center - http://www.kncpc.or.kr/en/main/main.asp
Public Procurement Service (PPS) - http://www.pps.go.kr/english/

Local Contact
Nathan Huh
Senior Commercial Specialist
U.S. Commercial Service, Korea
U.S. Embassy Seoul
188 Sejong-daero, Jongno-gu
Seoul 110-710 Korea
Tel: 82-2-397-4130
E-mail: Nathan.Huh@trade.gov

Semiconductors

ITA Code: N/A

Overview

Return to top

	2011	2012	2013 (E)	2014 (E)
Total Market Size	36,909.58	38,619.56	39,466.84	41,498.80
Total Local Production	57,422.44	60,293.56	63,308.24	66,473.66
Total Exports	54,763.56	59,692.28	65,661.51	67,631.36
Total Imports	34,250.70	38,018.28	41,820.10	42,656.50
Imports from the U.S.	13,700.28	15,207.31	16,728.04	17,062.60
Exchange Rate : 1USD	1,108	1,126	1,120.00	1,100.00

Source: Korea Communications Commission (KCC), Korea Electronics Association (KEA), and Ministry of Knowledge, Economy (MKE); Unit: USD million.

The semiconductor industry is one of the major IT industries in Korea. Both Samsung and SK Hynix cover 67.4 percent of memory chips (DRAM, NAND Flash) in the global market and Korea is also very competitive in the memory chip industry. However, memory chips are approximately only 20 percent of the total semiconductor industry.

Eighty percent of system semiconductor applications cover diverse wireless market demand for smart phones, tablet PCs, smart home appliances, automobiles, and aerospace, generating steady market growth. The market demand for system semiconductor major applications include communications applications (smart phones and others) and data processing applications (media tablets, solid state drives and others). This trend will continue as the mobile environment evolves.

Sub-Sector Best Prospects

Return to top

Analog Semiconductors -
Automobiles
Logic semiconductors for automobiles
32-bite Micro Controller Units (MCU)
Tire Pressure Monitoring Systems (TPMS)
Sensors for light, sound, pressure and temperature

System Semiconductors -
High-Definition Multimedia Interface (HDMI)
Display ports
Mobile High-Definition Links (MHL)

Opportunities

Return to top

As digital IT devices become smarter and smarter, they are evolving and working toward being able to recognize, imitate, interpret and act as if they are human beings. With the expansion of smart IT devices, the market demand for analog semiconductors is rapidly growing. Samsung manufactures image sensors and APs (Application Processors) and has more than 30 percent of global market share. However, Korean semiconductor manufacturers other than Samsung have an insignificant market share.

Korea is one of the major smart IT device, high-end TV (Digital TV, Smart TV and other high-end flat screen TV), and automobile manufacturing countries. These industries lead Korean market demand for system semiconductors and analog semiconductors. The major suppliers of analog and system semiconductors are from the U.S., Taiwan, Germany, and Japan.

Import Requirements

Korea is a party to the World Trade Organization Information Technology Agreement (ITA); as such, 92% of U.S. ICT products enjoy duty-free treatment into Korea. The remaining 8%, most of which would currently face eight percent tariffs in Korea, enter duty-free under the Korea-U.S. FTA (KORUS). These include radio and television parts, certain static converters, and some telecommunications apparatus.

Semiconductors have been duty-free under the Information Technology Agreement since 1996. However, next generation semiconductor chips, currently in development, may or may not be subject to duty. This issue is being handled at the Governments/ Authorities Meeting on Semiconductors (GAMS). Since 2000, GAMS has been an annual government-to-industry and government-to-government consultation between the World Semiconductor Council and the U.S., the EU, Japan and Korea.

There is no regulation applied to semiconductor chips, per se. However, when chips are utilized in electronic devices, the devices are subject to KC Mark conformity assessments. As the assessment procedure can be complicated, U.S. firms should consult with their Korean partners before exporting products containing these chips to the Korean market. The guidelines for the KC Mark can be found at: http://rra.go.kr/eng/approval/process/about.jsp

Web Resources   Return to top

Trade Shows
Korea Electronics Show - www.kes.org
Semicon Korea 2013 - www.semiconkorea.org
LED Korea 2013 - www.led-korea.org
World IT Show 2013 - http://www.worlditshow.co.kr/eng/index.php

Key Contacts
Ministry of Trade, Industry and Energy – www.motie.go.kr/language/eng/index.jsp
Korea Semiconductor Industry Association - https://www.ksia.or.kr/new/eng/main/
Korea Institute for Advancement of Technology -
http://www.kiat.or.kr/site/main/index/index002.jsp
Korea Electronics Association - http://www.gokea.org/neweiak/eng/

Local Contact
Ms. Alex Choi
Commercial Specialist
U.S. Commercial Service, Korea
U.S. Embassy Seoul
188, Sejong-daero, Chongno-gu
Seoul 110-710 Korea
Tel: 82-2-397-4466

E-mail: alex.choi@trade.gov
http://www.export.gov/southkorea

Travel and Tourism

SV TRA

Overview

	2011	**2012**	**2013 (estimated)**	**2014 (estimated)**
Outbound Travel	12,693,733	13,736,976	15,000,000	16,500,000
Outbound Travel to the U.S	1,145,216	1,283,000 (E)	1,385,000	1,482,000
Inbound Travel	9,794,796	11,140,028	12,300,000	13,500,000

Source: Korea Ministry of Culture and Tourism, tour.go.kr, Tourism Organization (KTO), U.S. Department of Commerce Office of Travel & Tourism Industries (USDOC, OTTI).

International travel is a rapidly-growing leisure activity for Koreans and offers opportunities for continued service industry growth. International travel by Koreans has been spurred by rising disposable incomes, gradual increases in leisure time, heightened globalization, and greater awareness of developments outside the Korean peninsula. Korea's per capita GDP rose to almost USD 32,400 in 2012, placing it securely in the ranks of middle-income countries. Korean consumer confidence has also increased gradually, including a rise in discretionary spending for such activities as overseas travel for business and leisure.

Continuing positive economic indicators, coupled with Korea's addition to countries included in the U.S. Visa Waiver Program (late 2008) and the recent U.S.-Korea Free Trade Agreement (KORUS FTA), which entered into force in March 2012, should help spur even more leisure and business-related travel to the U.S. Currently, 22% of Korean travel to the U.S. is for business purposes. Korean mass media is influenced by U.S. movies, advertising, popular culture, and the internet, which continue to stimulate interest in U.S. travel destinations.

Koreans overwhelmingly choose the U.S. as their non-Asian long-haul destination, primarily because of the diversity of tourism opportunities not generally available in Asia, including U.S.-style shopping, theme parks, cultural attractions in major U.S. cities, relatively inexpensive golf experiences, and U.S. National Parks.

According to the U.S. Department of Commerce, it is estimated that 1.28 million Koreans traveled to the U.S. in 2012. The increase is attributed to the stabilization of Korea's economy after the global financial crisis in 2008 and the Visa Waiver Program that Korea joined in 2008. Korea is currently the ninth-largest source of inbound travel to the U.S., behind Canada, Mexico, the United Kingdom, Japan, Germany, Brazil, China and France.

Sub-Sector Best Prospects

- Free and independent travelers
- Group package tours
- Family vacation packages
- Honeymoon packages
- Luxury packages catering to Korea's single, professional women, traveling for leisure

- Cultural tours and scenic/nature tour packages, especially designed for Korean travelers
- Educational travel

Opportunities Return to top

The U.S. is the leading non-Asian destination for Koreans as it offers a variety of activities, climates, and cultural experiences. U.S.-bound Koreans account for 9.3 percent of Korea's outbound market. Los Angeles, San Francisco, Las Vegas, and Seattle, followed by the New York-Washington, DC corridor, are the most popular destinations. Koreans use group tours or travel individually to visit friends and relatives. Group tours should focus on price-competitive products that entice travel agencies in Korea to sell these products. Korean travelers are generally interested in visiting museums, amusement parks, finding bargains at fashion outlets, purchasing OTC pharmaceuticals/vitamins and U.S. cosmetics, playing golf, and visiting restaurants and wineries.

To enter this market, travel and tourism entities should provide materials and guide experiences in the Korean language, continue knocking on doors, and cultivate relationships amongst travel agencies and other tour entities in Korea. There are approximately 9,000 tour agents in Korea and promotional information on the U.S. is urgently needed for developing this market.

A three-country USA Travel and Tourism Pavilion, including Korea, Taiwan and Japan, is being planned for March 2014. Contact CS Korea for more details.

Web Resources Return to top

Trade Events
May 24-26, 2013
Hanatour Exhibition

May 30-June 2, 2013
The 25th Korea World Travel Fair (KOTFA) - http://www.kotfa.co.kr/eng/main/main.htm

January 2014 (dates TBC)
Weddex Korea - http://www.weddex.com/html/weddexkorea/exhibit_intro.html

Key Contacts
Korea Tourism Organization   http://kto.visitkorea.or.kr/eng.kto
Ministry of Culture, Sports & Tourism   http://www.mcst.go.kr/english/index.jsp

Local Contact
Ms. Hae Lyong Kim
Commercial Specialist
U.S. Commercial Service, Korea
U.S. Embassy Seoul
188 Sejong-daero, Jongno-gu
Seoul 110-710 Korea
82-2-397-4459
E-mail: haelyong.kim@trade.gov

http://www.export.gov/southkorea

For information on agricultural products including bulk commodities or processed foods and the distribution channels in Korea, please see the US Department of Agriculture (USDA) Exporter Guide 2012.

When considering the Korean market, US food exporters should conduct preliminary research to determine if the market is appropriate for the product. Possible sources of market information include Korean importers, US state departments of agriculture, the US Agricultural Trade Office in Seoul and the US Department of Commerce. Lists of Korean importers, by product, can be obtained from the US Agricultural Trade Office, or through the Foreign Agricultural Service in Washington, D.C. The next step might include sending catalogues, brochures, product samples, and price lists to prospective importers as a way of introducing the company and products.

Once contact is established, it is advisable to visit the importer(s) in person, which will increase the seller's credibility with the Korean importer and give an opportunity to see the Korean market first hand. In Korea the clichés about "seeing is believing" and "one visit is worth a 1,000 e-mails" are especially true. Especially in Korea, there is no substitute for face-to-face meetings. The supplier or exporter should bring samples as well as product and company brochures including price lists, shipping dates, available quantities, and any other information needed for negotiating a contract. While information in English is acceptable, having it in Korean is especially helpful. A general overview of the firm in Korean is a good place to start.

The Seoul Food 2013 Exhibition presents an excellent opportunity to explore possible market opportunities in Korea. This show is a trade only show and targets importers, wholesalers, distributors, retailers, hotels, restaurants, food processors, media, etc.

Return to table of contents

Return to table of contents

Chapter 5: Trade Regulations, Customs and Standards

- Import Tariffs
- Trade Barriers
- Import Requirements and Documentation
- US Export Controls
- Temporary Entry
- Labeling and Marking Requirements
- Prohibited and Restricted Imports
- Customs Regulations and Contact Information
- Standards
- Trade Agreements
- Web Resources

Import Tariffs Return to top

The U.S.-Korea FTA was implemented on March 15, 2012. Prior to that, the average basic tariff on U.S. goods at about 7.9 percent and Duty rates were high on a large number of high-value agricultural and fisheries products. Now that the FTA is being implemented, 95% of tariffs on U.S. imports will be eliminated by March 15, 2017. The U.S. Department of Commerce's FTA Tariff Tool can help U.S. exporters identify the harmonized system number for their products and the associated tariff rates over the next ten years. Exporters can also contact the U.S. Agricultural Trade Office for specific information on agricultural tariff rates.

Korea also maintains a tariff quota system designed to stabilize domestic commodity markets. Customs duties can be adjusted every six months, within the limit of the basic rate, plus or minus 40 percent.

Korea has a flat 10 percent Value Added Tax on all imports and domestically manufactured goods. A special excise tax of 10-20 percent is also levied on the import of certain luxury items and durable consumer goods. Tariffs and taxes must be paid in Korean Won within 15 days after goods have cleared Customs.

Customs Valuation

Most duties are assessed on an ad valorem basis. Specific rates apply to some goods, while both ad valorem and specific rates apply to a few others. The dutiable value of imported goods is the cost, insurance, and freight (CIF) price at the time of import declaration.

Import duties are not assessed on capital goods and raw materials imported in connection with foreign investment projects. Authorization to import on a duty-free basis is usually accompanied by the Ministry of Strategy and Finance's approval of a foreign investment project.

For illustrative purposes, the following table demonstrates import duty and other taxes affecting the final import price:

Product Cost (Ex-Factory)	USD 100.00
Insurance and Freight (C&F)	USD 15.00
CIF Price	USD 115.00
Import Tariff/Duty (valuation CIF + VAT)	USD 5.00
Value Added Tax (VAT)	USD 12.30
Final Imported Price	USD 132.30

Trade Barriers Return to top

Korea continues a process of economic liberalization and deregulation, but the Republic of Korea government (ROKG) has yet to adopt a fully laissez-faire policy where the economy and trade are concerned. The U.S. Embassy, in cooperation with the American Chamber of Commerce (AmCham) in Korea, works actively to lift or loosen the many regulatory trade restrictions that currently exist.

Overcoming regulatory barriers to trade is also a major focus of the U.S.-Korea FTA. Transparency, due process, public comment/appeals procedures, and timely and written administrative procedures are among the topics that were addressed and agreed to and which affect a number of the sector-specific elements to the Agreement.

Information on specific trade barriers in Korea, including agricultural products (such as restrictions on rice imports) is available in the 2012 National Trade Estimate Report on Foreign Trade Barriers for Korea.

Import Requirements and Documentation Return to top

For companies exporting to the Republic of Korea, the following shipping documents are required to clear Korean Customs:

COMMERCIAL INVOICE: An original invoice and two copies must be presented with the shipping documents and must include total value, unit value, quantity, marks, product description and shipping from/to information.

CERTIFICATE OF ORIGIN: Prior to implementation of the KORUS FTA, a Certificate of Origin, in duplicate, was required for some products. Exporters are encouraged to discuss shipping document requirements with their respective importer.

An importer may claim preferential treatment under the KORUS FTA in order to receive the lower tariff. The importer can do this by providing written or electronic certification to Korean Customs from the manufacturer, the exporter or the importer. The importer is required to retain all documents demonstrating that the good qualifies as a U.S.-origin good for five years.

Self-certification of origin by the producer or exporter is normally the basis for deciding that the good qualifies for preferential tariff rates. If the certification is in English, an official translation into Korean must be presented by the importer to Korean Customs. A certification may be made for a single shipment or for multiple shipments of identical goods, for up to twelve months, by specifying this in the certification. The importer submits the certification to Korean Customs, in writing or electronically, including at least the following information:

a. Name and contact information for the certifying person
b. The importer
c. The exporter
d. The producer of the good
e. Harmonized System Tariff classification and description of the good
f. Information demonstrating that the good originates from the United States. This can be satisfied by either:
    i. The producer's written or electronic certification that the product meets KORUS FTA origin requirements; or
    ii. The producer's or exporter's knowledge that the good meets KORUS FTA origin requirements.
g. Date of the certification
h. In the case of a blanket certification, the period that the certification covers.

PACKING LISTS: Two copies are required.

BILL OF LADING: A clean bill of lading identifying the name of the shipper, the name and address of the consignee, the name of the port of destination, description of the cargo, a price list of freight and insurance charges (CIF), and attestation of carrier's acceptance on board for the goods is sufficient. There are no regulations pertaining to the form of the bill of lading nor the number of bills of lading required to clear customs. As bills of lading are for ocean and overland cargos, the airway bill of lading replaces the bill of lading for air cargo shipments.

MARITIME INSURANCE: Under the Incoterms (shipping terms) agreed to by the parties in a transaction, if the exporter is responsible for insurance, a marine insurance policy or insurance certificate is required.

SPECIAL DOCUMENTATION:

Information related to the need of special documentation for food and agricultural commodities, including sanitary-phytosanitary certificates and other agricultural documentation, can be found on the USDA/Animal Plant Health Inspection Service (APHIS) website at: http://www.aphis.usda.gov/import_export/index.shtml.

An overview of Korean import requirements for food is contained in the FAS Korea annual agriculture export guide at:
http://gain.fas.usda.gov/Recent%20GAIN%20Publications/Food%20and%20Agricultural%20Import%20Regulations%20and%20Standards%20-%20Certification_Seoul_Korea%20-%20Republic%20of_1-17-2013.pdf

Additional detailed information about import requirements and documentation needs for agricultural and food products (including biotechnology products) are included in the import requirements report at:

Additional information on how the KORUS Free Trade Agreement affects duty rates can be found on the Food and Agricultural Import Regulations and Standards (FAIRS) report for Korea. The Korean Food and Drug Administration (KFDA) provides information on maximum residue levels and import procedures on the KFDA website. Additional detail on the maximum residue limits allowed by Korean food authorities and reports on import requirements for organic products are also available on the FAS website. Exporters of organic products should also review the FAS report on Korean regulatory requirements for transgenic content in organic processed food products.

Current information on which U.S. livestock and poultry products are eligible for export to the Korean market can be found on the website of the Food Safety and Inspection Service of the U.S. Department of Agriculture. This website also provides guidance on the documents Korea requires for livestock product shipments destined for Korea.

All commodities, except rice, can be freely imported, subject to special registrations and import approvals for categories like pharmaceuticals, medical devices, and cosmetics. The Government of Korea has stipulated requirements and procedures for importing certain products including registration, standards and safety and efficacy testing to ensure the protection of public health and sanitation, national security, safety, and the environment. Typically, health or safety related products, such as pharmaceuticals and medicines, require additional testing or certification by recommended organizations before clearing Customs. Medical device and pharmaceutical exporters must have their products registered with the Korea Food and Drug Administration and can only be imported by licensed importers which have been certified by a KFDA authorized body. In addition, special items defined by the Ministry of Trade, Industry and Energy (MOTIE) in its Annual Trade Plan require approval by the Minister. In most cases, the supplier's qualified local agent completes the registration process.

US Export Controls   Return to top

The Department of Commerce, Bureau of Industry and Security (BIS) develops, implements, and interprets U.S. export control policy for dual-use commodities, software, and technology. Dual-use items subject to BIS regulatory jurisdiction have predominantly commercial uses, but may also have military applications. For basic information on U.S. export controls, please visit the following website: http://www.bis.doc.gov/licensing/exportingbasics.htm. For information on export controls administered by other U.S. Government agencies, please visit http://www.bis.doc.gov/About/reslinks.htm.

Temporary Entry   Return to top

Korea has three kinds of bonded areas where goods can temporarily enter Korea for storage, manufacture, processing, sale, construction, or exhibit without going through Customs clearance. The three types of bonded areas are: 1) designated bonded areas (designated storage sites and Customs inspection zones); 2) patent bonded areas (bonded warehouses, bonded factories, bonded exhibition sites, bonded construction sites, and bonded sales shops); and, 3) comprehensive bonded areas (all five activities of patent bonded areas can be performed comprehensively in the same place). Duties are payable only when goods are cleared through Customs.

The period for which goods may be stored in a designated bonded warehouse is six months and a patent bonded warehouse is one year. Storage fees are relatively high, and the availability of a bonded warehouse to maintain inventories is limited. The storage period does not apply to the storage of live animals or plants, perishable merchandise, or other commodities that may cause damage to other merchandise or to the warehouse. The Collector of Customs bears no responsibility for goods while they are stored in Customs facilities.

Comprehensive bonded areas have no time limit for storage. Hence, storage, manufacturing, processing, building, sales and exhibition can be comprehensively carried out. U.S. exporters can store shipped goods and still maintain title until they are cleared through Customs. Korea's customs laws specify that any person who wishes to establish a bonded warehouse shall obtain a license from the director of each Customs Zone. Applications must include the name of the bonded warehouse, location, structure, numbers and sizes of buildings, storage capacity and types of products to be stored. In addition, articles of incorporation and corporate registration must be submitted, when applicable.

Goods entering Korea for exhibition purposes must be stored in a bonded area. For example, the Korea Exhibition Center (COEX) is a bonded area. Exhibition goods will be held without charge at COEX during the exhibition period, after which they must be either: 1) reshipped directly out of Korea without payment of duty; 2) presented at Customs for payment of regular duty on value declared at time of entry; or 3) transferred to the Seoul Customs house bonded storage area. Goods stored in a bonded warehouse may incur storage costs, customs brokerage charges, local transportation costs and moving equipment fees.

Korean Customs has simplified clearance procedures for goods with particular purposes (samples, goods for warranty and non-warranty repair).

The ATA Carnet is an international customs document that a traveler may use to temporarily import certain goods into a country without having to engage in the customs formalities usually required for the importation of goods, and without having to pay duty or value-added taxes on the goods. Korea allows for the temporary importation of commercial samples, professional equipment and certain advertising materials by a non-resident individual. By definition, a temporary import is for six months or less. Therefore, a carnet is valid for a maximum of six months in Korea.

For more detailed information about guidelines for temporary entry of items into Korea, please visit the Korea Customs website.

Labeling and Marking Requirements   Return to top

Korea has specific labeling and marking requirements for certain products, such as pharmaceuticals, as well as for organic and functional food and food produced through biotechnology. Details regarding these and other general labeling and marking requirements can be found on the Foreign Agricultural Service website pertaining to food and agriculture import requirements at:

http://gain.fas.usda.gov/Recent%20GAIN%20Publications/Food%20and%20Agricultural
%20Import%20Regulations%20and%20Standards%20-
%20Narrative_Seoul_Korea%20-%20Republic%20of_1-23-2013.pdf

Country of origin labeling is required for commercial shipments entering Korea. The Korean Customs Service (KCS) publishes a list of country of origin labeling requirements by Harmonized System Code number. Please visit Labeling and Marking. The usage of "Assembled in *Country*" was allowed starting October 2010.

The Korean Ministry of Trade, Industry and Energy (formerly the Ministry of Knowledge Economy) began issuing the KC Mark for items that fall under its jurisdiction. Formerly, some 13 mandatory marks were issued, many which overlapped in testing procedures and functions. The consolidation of these marks into the KC Mark ensures that companies, both Korean and foreign agencies, will save time and costs due to reduced redundancies introduced into this new system. To learn more about this, click "KC Mark" (this site has an English version, but the initial page is in Korean).

Further labeling and marking requirements for specific products, such as pharmaceutical and food products, are covered by specific regulations from the Korean Government agencies responsible for these items. Korean language labels, except for country of origin markings that must be shown at the time of customs clearance, can be attached locally on products in the bonded area, either before or after clearance.

Details regarding labeling and marking regulations for food and agricultural products can be found on the Foreign Agricultural Service website in the Food and Agriculture regulatory guide at:
http://gain.fas.usda.gov/Recent%20GAIN%20Publications/Food%20and%20Agricultural
%20Import%20Regulations%20and%20Standards%20-
%20Narrative_Seoul_Korea%20-%20Republic%20of_1-23-2013.pdf

Prohibited and Restricted Imports   Return to top

Guns, narcotics, pornography, subversive material, treasonous material and counterfeit goods or materials are prohibited entry into Korea.

Please visit the Bureau of Industry and Security website at: http://www.bis.doc.gov/ for detailed information about export controls to the Republic of Korea. The Korean Customs Service also maintains a list of prohibited imports to the Republic of Korea.

Customs Regulations and Contact Information   Return to top

Korea maintains an import declaration system that allows for the immediate release of goods upon acceptance of an import declaration filed without defect. With the exception of high-risk items related to public health and sanitation, national security, and the environment, which often require additional documentation and technical tests, goods imported by companies with no record of trade law violations are released upon the acceptance of the import declaration without Customs inspection. The Korean Customs Service's Electronic Data Interchange (EDI) system for paperless import clearance allows importers to make an import declaration by computer without visiting the Customs House.

Import declarations may be filed at the Customs House before a vessel enters a port or before the goods are unloaded into bonded areas. In both cases, goods are released directly from the port without being stored in a bonded area, if the import declaration is accepted.

Exporters can file an export notice to Korean Customs by computer-based shipping documents at the time of export clearance. All commodities can be freely exported unless they are included on the negative list.

To view Customs regulations, please go to the website below:

Korea Customs Service
Telephone: 82-42-472-2196
Fax: 82-42-481-7969
E-mail: kcstcd@customs.go.kr
http://english.customs.go.kr/

Standards   Return to top

- Overview
- Standards Organizations
- Conformity Assessment
- Product Certification
- Accreditation
- Publication of Technical Regulations
- Contacts

Overview   Return to top

The Korean Government adopted the ISO 9000 system (modified as the KSA 9000) as the official standard system in April 1992. The Korean Agency for Technology and Standards (KATS) continues to work to make Korean standards similar to international standards. The Korean Industrial Standardization Act requires 60 days' notice before implementing new standards. Whenever there is a change in standards, the government is required to notify the WTO's Committee on Technical Barriers to Trade (TBT). To be alerted on these notifications, please visit http://www.nist.gov/notifyus.

Details regarding standards and import regulations for food and agricultural products can be found on the Foreign Agricultural Service website and in the Food and Agricultural Import Regulations and Standards (FAIRS) report for Korea.

Standards Organizations   Return to top

The Korean Agency for Technology and Standards (KATS) develops standards for most industrial products in Korea. The agency consults with other private organizations to develop standards and certification requirements.

The Korean Food and Drug Administration (KFDA) establishes standards for research, new product evaluation, test method development, product monitoring for food, medical devices, pharmaceuticals and radiation technology distributed within Korea.

The Telecommunications Technology Association (TTA) covers telecommunications, information technology, radio communications and broadcasting. The Association establishes industry standards and has been instrumental in creating the current Korean Information and Communication Standards. TTA also collaborates with international and national standards organizations, such as ITU and other organizations.

NIST Notify U.S. Service

Member countries of the World Trade Organization (WTO) are required under the Agreement on Technical Barriers to Trade (TBT) to report to the WTO all proposed technical regulations which could affect trade with other member countries. **Notify U.S.** is a free, web-based e-mail subscription service that offers the opportunity to review and comment on proposed foreign technical regulations that may affect access to international markets. Register online at internet URL: http://www.nist.gov/notifyus/.

Conformity Assessment   Return to top

KATS establishes guidelines for government and private sector institutions to perform reliability assessment and certification. It also performs market surveillance on Korean Certification (KC)-marked products and penalizes products that do not meet KC requirements.

Korea is a signatory to the GATT Standards Agreement. As such, Korea must apply open procedures for the adoption of standards, announce recommended standards, provide sufficient information on proposed standards or alterations in standards, and allow sufficient time for countries and other stakeholders to comment on proposed standards implementation.

Product Certification   Return to top

KATS issues certification marks for new technologies and recognizes quality products manufactured by Korean companies mainly to promote exports and also imports into Korea. On July 1, 2009, KATS began issuing the KC Mark for items that fall under its jurisdiction. Information related to the KC Mark in English can be found at the American National Standards Institute (ANSI) website at: http://www.standardsportal.org/usa_kr/e/conformity_assessment/ca_marks_used_in_kor ea.aspx. The KC Mark is required to reduce and minimize repetitive testing at various ministries and agencies. The consolidation of these marks ensures that companies, both Korean and foreign, will save time and costs due to reduced redundancies introduced into this new system.

Accreditation   Return to top

Established in December 1992, the Korea Laboratory Accreditation Scheme (KOLAS) is the government accreditation body under the KATS Department of Technology and Standards Planning. Additional information and accreditation bodies can be found under the KOLAS website at http://www.kolas.go.kr/english/.

Publication of Technical Regulations   Return to top

Revised or new standards or technical regulations are published by the Korean Agency for Technology and Standards (KATS) and made available at http://www.kats.go.kr/en_kats/. The articles are generally published only in Korean. All proposed or newly-revised/established technical regulations are consolidated on this site.

Proposed revisions or establishment of regulations in Korea are made by the Director of Technical Regulations via the website: http://www.kats.go.kr/en_kats/. A public meeting consisting of lawmakers as well as relevant private/public industry organizations is held to comment on proposed regulations. Contact the U.S. Embassy, Commercial Section for assistance with revised or new standards.

Contacts Return to top

Korean Agency for Technology and Standards (KATS)
http://www.kats.go.kr/en_kats/

Korean Food and Drug Administration (KFDA)
http://www.kfda.go.kr/eng/index.do

Korean Laboratory Accreditation Scheme (KOLAS)
www.kolas.go.kr

Trade Agreements Return to top

The Republic of Korea and the United States implemented the Korea-U.S. Free Trade Agreement on March 15, 2012. The Agreement is the largest FTA negotiated by the United States since NAFTA. For more information about the KORUS FTA, please visit http://www.ustr.gov/trade-agreements/free-trade-agreements/korus-fta.

The Republic of Korea is a member of the Asia-Pacific Economic Cooperation (APEC) forum. One goal of APEC, as outlined in its 1994 declaration, is to establish a Free Trade Area among its member countries by the year 2020. Substantive principles of the APEC forum include investment liberalization, tariff reduction, deregulation, government procurement, and strengthening IPR protection. Korea was the host country for APEC in 2005.

Korea has Free Trade Agreements with Chile, Singapore, European Union and the European Free Trade Association (Norway, Switzerland, Iceland and Liechtenstein). More information on EU-Korea FTA can be found on the European Union website at http://ec.europa.eu/trade/creating-opportunities/bilateral-relations/countries/korea/.

Korea also signed a framework agreement with the Association of South East Asian Nations (ASEAN) that led to an FTA in goods by the end of 2006 and other areas by the end of 2008.

The Republic of Korea is a member of the World Trade Organization (WTO) and has signed subsidiary agreements including TRIPs (Trade Related Aspects of Intellectual Property) and the Government Procurement Agreement. Korea has been a member of the Organization for Economic Cooperation and Development (OECD) since December 1996.

U.S. Department of Commerce, Commercial Service, Korea
http://export.gov/southkorea/

U.S. Agricultural Trade Office in Seoul
www.atoseoul.com

U.S. Department of Agriculture
http://www.usda.gov

USDA Agriculture Exporters Guide
http://www.fas.usda.gov/agx/exporter_assistance.asp

USDA Animal Plant and Health Inspection Service (APHIS)
www.aphis.usda.gov

USDA Food Safety and Inspection Service
http://www.fsis.usda.gov/Regulations_&_Policies/Republic_of_Korea_Requirements/index.asp

Foreign Agricultural Service (FAS), U.S. Department of Agriculture (Attaché Reports)
www.fas.usda.gov

American Chamber of Commerce Korea
http://www.amchamkorea.org

Department of Commerce, Bureau of Industry and Security
http://www.bis.doc.gov/

Annual National Trade Estimate Report
http://www.ustr.gov/sites/default/files/Korea_0.pdf

Korean Agency for Technology and Standards (KATS)
http://www.kats.go.kr/english/index.asp

Korea Customs Service
http://english.customs.go.kr/

Korean Food and Drug Administration (KFDA)
http://eng.kfda.go.kr/index.php

Korean Laboratory Accreditation Scheme (KOLAS)
http://www.kolas.go.kr/english/

Telecommunications Technology Association (TTA)
http://www.tta.or.kr/English/index.jsp

Return to table of contents

Return to table of contents

Chapter 6: Investment Climate

For background information on the investment climate of the country, please click on the link below to the U.S. Embassy in Seoul Notes.

http://seoul.usembassy.gov/business_0612.html

Additional Notes on Corruption Return to top

Corruption, including bribery, raises the costs and risks of doing business. Corruption has a corrosive impact on both market opportunities overseas for U.S. companies and the broader business climate. It also deters international investment, stifles economic growth and development, distorts prices, and undermines the rule of law.

It is important for U.S. companies, irrespective of their size, to assess the business climate in the relevant market in which they will be operating or investing, and to have an effective compliance program or measures to prevent and detect corruption, including foreign bribery. U.S. individuals and firms operating or investing in foreign markets should take the time to become familiar with the relevant anticorruption laws of both the foreign country and the United States in order to properly comply with them, and where appropriate, they should seek the advice of legal counsel.

The U.S. Government seeks to level the global playing field for U.S. businesses by encouraging other countries to take steps to criminalize their own companies' acts of corruption, including bribery of foreign public officials, by requiring them to uphold their obligations under relevant international conventions. A U.S. firm that believes a competitor is seeking to use bribery of a foreign public official to secure a contract should bring this to the attention of appropriate U.S. agencies, as noted below.

U.S. Foreign Corrupt Practices Act: In 1977, the United States enacted the Foreign Corrupt Practices Act (FCPA), which makes it unlawful for a U.S. person, and certain foreign issuers of securities, to make a corrupt payment to foreign public officials for the purpose of obtaining or retaining business for or with, or directing business to, any person. The FCPA also applies to foreign firms and persons who take any act in furtherance of such a corrupt payment while in the United States. For more detailed information on the FCPA, see the FCPA Lay-Person's Guide at:
http://www.justice.gov/criminal/fraud/

Other Instruments: It is U.S. Government policy to promote good governance, including host country implementation and enforcement of anti-corruption laws and policies pursuant to their obligations under international agreements. Since enactment of the FCPA, the United States has been instrumental to the expansion of the international framework to fight corruption. Several significant components of this framework are the OECD Convention on Combating Bribery of Foreign Public Officials in International Business Transactions (OECD Antibribery Convention), the United Nations Convention against Corruption (UN Convention), the Inter-American Convention against Corruption (OAS Convention), the Council of Europe Criminal and Civil Law Conventions, and a growing list of U.S. free trade agreements. Generally all countries prohibit the bribery and solicitation of their public officials.

OECD Antibribery Convention: The OECD Antibribery Convention entered into force in February 1999. As of March 2009, there are 38 parties to the Convention including the United States (see http://www.oecd.org/dataoecd/59/13/40272933.pdf). Major exporters China, India, and Russia are not parties, although the U.S. Government strongly endorses their eventual accession to the Convention. The Convention obligates the Parties to criminalize bribery of foreign public officials in the conduct of international business. The United States meets its international obligations under the OECD Antibribery Convention through the U.S. FCPA. South Korea is a member country of the OECD convention.

UN Convention: The UN Anticorruption Convention entered into force on December 14, 2005, and there are 158 parties to it as of November 2011 (see http://www.unodc.org/unodc/en/treaties/CAC/signatories.html). The UN Convention is the first global comprehensive international anticorruption agreement. The UN Convention requires countries to establish criminal and other offences to cover a wide range of acts of corruption. The UN Convention goes beyond previous anticorruption instruments, covering a broad range of issues ranging from basic forms of corruption such as bribery and solicitation, embezzlement, trading in influence to the concealment and laundering of the proceeds of corruption. The Convention contains transnational business bribery provisions that are functionally similar to those in the OECD Antibribery Convention and contains provisions on private sector auditing and books and records requirements. Other provisions address matters such as prevention, international cooperation, and asset recovery. The Republic of Korea is a member nation of the UN Convention.

OAS Convention: In 1996, the Member States of the Organization of American States (OAS) adopted the first international anticorruption legal instrument, the Inter-American Convention against Corruption (OAS Convention), which entered into force in March 1997. The OAS Convention, among other things, establishes a set of preventive measures against corruption, provides for the criminalization of certain acts of corruption, including transnational bribery and illicit enrichment, and contains a series of provisions to strengthen the cooperation between its States Parties in areas such as mutual legal assistance and technical cooperation. As of December 2009, the OAS Convention has 34 parties (see http://www.oas.org/juridico/english/Sigs/b-58.html). The Republic of Korea is not a member of the OAS Convention.

Council of Europe Criminal Law and Civil Law Conventions: Many European countries are parties to either the Council of Europe (CoE) Criminal Law Convention on Corruption, the Civil Law Convention, or both. The Criminal Law Convention requires criminalization of a wide range of national and transnational conduct, including bribery, money-laundering, and account offenses. It also incorporates provisions on liability of legal persons and witness protection. The Civil Law Convention includes provisions on compensation for damage relating to corrupt acts, whistleblower protection, and validity of contracts, inter alia. The Group of States against Corruption (GRECO) was established in 1999 by the CoE to monitor compliance with these and related anti-corruption standards. Currently, GRECO comprises 49 member States (48 European countries and the United States). As of December 2011, the Criminal Law Convention has 43 parties and the Civil Law Convention has 34 (see www.coe.int/greco.) The Republic of Korea is not a member of the Council of Europe Conventions.

Free Trade Agreements: While it is U.S. Government policy to include anticorruption provisions in free trade agreements (FTAs) that it negotiates with its trading partners, the anticorruption provisions have evolved over time. The most recent FTAs negotiated now require trading partners to criminalize "active bribery" of public officials (offering bribes to any public official must be made a criminal offense, both domestically and trans-nationally) as well as domestic "passive bribery" (solicitation of a bribe by a domestic official). All U.S. FTAs may be found at the U.S. Trade Representative Website: http://www.ustr.gov/trade-agreements/free-trade-agreements. The Republic of Korea has a free trade agreement (FTA) in place with the United States, the KORUS FTA, which came into force on March 15, 2012.

Local Laws: U.S. firms should familiarize themselves with local anticorruption laws, and, where appropriate, seek legal counsel. While the U.S. Department of Commerce cannot provide legal advice on local laws, the Department's U.S. and Foreign Commercial Service can provide assistance with navigating the host country's legal system and obtaining a list of local legal counsel.

Assistance for U.S. Businesses: The U.S. Department of Commerce offers several services to aid U.S. businesses seeking to address business-related corruption issues. For example, the U.S. and Foreign Commercial Service can provide services that may assist U.S. companies in conducting their due diligence as part of the company's overarching compliance program when choosing business partners or agents overseas. The U.S. Foreign and Commercial Service can be reached directly through its offices in every major U.S. and foreign city, or through its Website at www.trade.gov/cs.

The Departments of Commerce and State provide worldwide support for qualified U.S. companies bidding on foreign government contracts through the Commerce Department's Advocacy Center and State's Office of Commercial and Business Affairs. Problems, including alleged corruption by foreign governments or competitors, encountered by U.S. companies in seeking such foreign business opportunities can be brought to the attention of appropriate U.S. government officials, including local embassy personnel and through the Department of Commerce Trade Compliance Center "Report A Trade Barrier" Website at tcc.export.gov/Report_a_Barrier/index.asp.

Guidance on the U.S. FCPA: The Department of Justice's (DOJ) FCPA Opinion Procedure enables U.S. firms and individuals to request a statement of the Justice Department's present enforcement intentions under the anti-bribery provisions of the FCPA regarding any proposed business conduct. The details of the opinion procedure are available on DOJ's Fraud Section Website at www.justice.gov/criminal/fraud/fcpa. Although the Department of Commerce has no enforcement role with respect to the FCPA, it supplies general guidance to U.S. exporters who have questions about the FCPA and about international developments concerning the FCPA. For further information, see the Office of the Chief Counsel for International Counsel, U.S. Department of Commerce, Website, at http://www.ogc.doc.gov/trans_anti_bribery.html. More general information on the FCPA is available at the Websites listed below.

Exporters and investors should be aware that generally all countries prohibit the bribery of their public officials, and prohibit their officials from soliciting bribes under domestic laws. Most countries are required to criminalize such bribery and other acts of corruption by virtue of being parties to various international conventions discussed above.

Public sector corruption, including bribery of public officials, remains a challenge for U.S. firms operating in South Korea. To learn more, click http://seoul.usembassy.gov/business_0612.html.

Anti-Corruption Resources

Some useful resources for individuals and companies regarding combating corruption in global markets include the following:

- Information about the U.S. Foreign Corrupt Practices Act (FCPA), including a "Lay-Person's Guide to the FCPA" is available at the U.S. Department of Justice's Website at: http://www.justice.gov/criminal/fraud/fcpa.

- Information about the OECD Antibribery Convention including links to national implementing legislation and country monitoring reports is available at: http://www.oecd.org/department/0,3355,en_2649_34859_1_1_1_1_1,00.html. See also new Antibribery Recommendation and Good Practice Guidance Annex for companies: http://www.oecd.org/dataoecd/11/40/44176910.pdf.

- General information about anticorruption initiatives, such as the OECD Convention and the FCPA, including translations of the statute into several languages, is available at the Department of Commerce Office of the Chief Counsel for International Commerce Website: http://www.ogc.doc.gov/trans_anti_bribery.html.

- Transparency International (TI) publishes an annual Corruption Perceptions Index (CPI). The CPI measures the perceived level of public-sector corruption in 180 countries and territories around the world. The CPI is available at: http://www.transparency.org/policy_research/surveys_indices/cpi/2009. TI also publishes an annual *Global Corruption Report* which provides a systematic evaluation of the state of corruption around the world. It includes an in-depth analysis of a focal theme, a series of country reports that document major corruption related events and developments from all continents and an overview of the latest research findings on anti-corruption diagnostics and tools. See http://www.transparency.org/publications/gcr.

- The World Bank Institute publishes Worldwide Governance Indicators (WGI). These indicators assess six dimensions of governance in 213 countries, including Voice and Accountability, Political Stability and Absence of Violence, Government Effectiveness, Regulatory Quality, Rule of Law and Control of Corruption. See http://info.worldbank.org/governance/wgi/index.asp. The World Bank Business Environment and Enterprise Performance Surveys may also be of interest and are available at: http://data.worldbank.org/data-catalog/BEEPS.

- The World Economic Forum publishes the *Global Enabling Trade Report*, which presents the rankings of the Enabling Trade Index, and includes an assessment of the transparency of border administration (focused on bribe payments and corruption) and a separate segment on corruption and the regulatory environment. See http://www.weforum.org/s?s=global+enabling+trade+report.

- Additional country information related to corruption can be found in the U.S. State Department's annual *Human Rights Report* available at http://www.state.gov/g/drl/rls/hrrpt/.

- Global Integrity, a nonprofit organization, publishes its annual *Global Integrity Report*, which provides indicators for 106 countries with respect to governance and anti-corruption. The report highlights the strengths and weaknesses of national level anti-corruption systems. The report is available at: http://report.globalintegrity.org/.

Return to table of contents

Chapter 7: Trade and Project Financing

- How Do I Get Paid (Methods of Payment)
- How Does the Banking System Operate
- Financial Services and KORUS FTA
- Foreign-Exchange Controls
- U.S. Banks and Local Correspondent Banks
- Project Financing
- Web Resources

How Do I Get Paid (Methods of Payment)   Return to top

The Korean financial system is frequently hard-pressed to meet the demand for financing and capital for international commercial transactions. This is mainly attributed to banks holding BIS (Bank for International Settlement Reserves) capital adequacy ratios above the 10 percent required, and by being stricter on loan requirements for SMEs and small businesses, given significant personal household debt. Foreign companies in start-up operations with a Korean partner often need to invest financial resources for the joint venture, while their Korean partner makes in-kind investments, i.e., land or facilities, for their share of equity. Joint-venture companies and foreign firms often work with branches of foreign banks for local-currency financing, although the branches of foreign banks control a small portion of available Korean Won.

Sources of Korean Won financing have included domestic commercial banks, regional banks, and specialized banks, including the Korea Development Bank, the National Agricultural Cooperative Federation, the Industrial Bank of Korea (IBK), and the Korea Housing Bank.

Korea's major international banks offer services for all types of international trade payment methods. When you engaged in business activities with a customer overseas, knowing how to collect payment on an overseas sales transaction is the single most critical factor for SME business owners who aspire to expand their international business operations.

There are basically three ways to get paid overseas:

- Sight and deferred payment Letters of Credit (L/C),
- Documents against Acceptance (D/A) and Documents against Payment (D/P), and
- Open Account Transactions.

D/A and L/Cs are forms of extended credit in which the importer makes no payment for the goods until the date called for in the L/C.

D/P is similar to D/A except that the importer cannot clear the goods from customs prior to making payment. In some cases an importer can clear goods prior to payment under a sight L/C. L/C transactions generally follow standard international Uniform Customs and Practice (UCP) codes.

CS Korea recommends that U.S. companies consider dealing on a confirmed L/C credit basis with new and even familiar customers. A confirmed L/C through a U.S. bank is recommended because it prevents unwanted changes to the original L/C, and it places responsibility for collection on the banks rather than on the seller. Once a business relationship has strengthened over time, use of payment mechanisms other than L/Cs can be employed.

To reduce risk of nonpayment, U.S. companies may also contact credit rating agencies, which can provide fee-based corporate information to evaluate the financial credibility of Korean companies. Dun & Bradstreet Korea (https://www.dnb.com/english/contactus/index.htm), the Korea Investors Service (http://www.kisrating.com/eng/), and the Korean Information Service are known to provide fee-based credit rating services in Korea.

CS Korea can provide valuable information, including a company's credit standing, through our fee-based International Company Profile Service http://export.gov/southkorea/servicesforuscompanies/icp/index.asp. The Korean Commercial Arbitration Board http://www.kcab.or.kr/servlet/kcab_adm/memberauth/5000, and private collection agencies can provide arbitration and collection services. The KCAB is staffed with counselors who advise U.S. companies on contract guidelines.

Whatever payment terms are agreed upon, make sure they are understood by all parties and that your client, representative or contact signs a mutually agreed document. Payment terms must be agreed to in advance. It is rarely wise to sell on open account to a brand new customer.

How Does the Banking System Operate   Return to top

Korea's financial system consists of banking and non-bank financial institutions. The Financial Supervisory Commission (FSC: http://www.fsc.go.kr/eng/) and the Financial Supervisory Service (FSS: http://english.fss.or.kr/fss/en/main.jsp), its regulatory arm, are responsible for supervising and examining all banks, including specialized and government-owned banks, as well as securities and insurance companies. The FSC has played a key role in financial restructuring and has strengthened the regulatory and supervisory framework governing the entire financial sector. Oversight standards are improving, but they will need more time to meet international standards.

Korea's 18 largest banks (the four largest hold approximately 70% of market share) in 2011 (4Q) reported a BIS average capital adequacy ratio of 13.94% and a Tier I capital ratio of 11.06%. These ratios are higher than required under Basel II (Basel II is the international agreement requiring banks to maintain adequate capital ratios in anticipation of global slowdown or financial crises). This Basel II ratio is in accord with the Government of Korea's efforts to strengthen the quality and quantity of bank capital, while being more conservative given the country's reliance on trade, any future global economic downturn, and other ongoing economic concerns in the Euro Zone.

Financial Services and KORUS FTA   Return to top

With the passage (Fall 2011) and the March 15, 2012 implementation of the KORUS FTA, the U.S. financial service industry can expect new and unprecedented access to the Korean market. Financial service commitments outlined in the KORUS FTA are some of the most progressive commitments made with any U.S. trade partner to date. The Agreement locks in standards, regulations, and commitments that increase the transparency, predictability, and cost-efficiency for operating in the Korean financial services market.

Some of the financial service commitments inherent in this Agreement include:

- Language allowing for cross-border data flow and giving U.S.-based "back-office" support to U.S. firms with operations in Korea. This commitment has a two-year phase-in period, designed to identify, review, and modify data transfer practices to ensure protections in Korea that are no less stringent than those in the U.S.
- Permitting U.S. financial institutions the ability to establish or acquire financial institutions in Korea and choose the corporate form that best meets their business needs
- Encouraging Korea to implement several reforms that would contribute to the transparency of rules and procedures, including regional integration of data processing.

Consult: http://www.uskoreafta.org/sites/default/files/Financial-Services-KORUS.pdf.

Foreign-Exchange Controls Return to top

Korea has liberalized foreign exchange controls in line with OECD benchmarks. A foreign firm that invests under the terms of the Foreign Capital Promotion Act (FCPA: http://untreaty.un.org/cod/avl/pdf/ls/Shin_RelDocs.pdf) is permitted to remit a substantial portion of its profits, providing it submits an audited financial statement to its foreign exchange bank.

To withdraw capital, a stock valuation report issued by a recognized securities company or the Korean Appraisal Board must be presented. Foreign companies not investing under the FCPA must repatriate funds through authorized foreign exchange banks after obtaining government approval. Although Korea does not routinely limit the repatriation of funds, it reserves the right to do so in exceptional circumstances, such as in situations which may harm its international balance of payments, cause excessive fluctuations in interest or exchange rates, or threaten the stability of its domestic financial markets. To date, the Korean government has had no instance of limiting repatriation for these reasons, even during and after the 1997-98 financial crisis.

The Bank of Korea has detailed information about foreign-exchange control policies in Korea. Consult: http://eng.bok.or.kr/.

U.S. Banks and Local Correspondent Banks Return to top

For a list of major U.S. and Korean banks in Korea, consult:
http://export.gov/southkorea/usefullinks/majoruskoreanbanks/index.aspgov/korea/en/bankcontacts.html.

Project financing (PF) is designed to facilitate funding of large-scale projects. The concept was first introduced in Korea to finance a highway construction project between Seoul and the Incheon International Airport. The government's decision to introduce this financing technique was prompted by the need to boost domestic demand by stimulating investments in large-scale projects, including housing construction and social infrastructure facilities.

Most of Korea's social overhead capital (SOC) projects are funded through PF. PF is also used for the financing of private sector projects, to include real estate development and buy-outs of financially troubled companies. Several Korean and foreign banks provide PF and offer venture capital investment programs for social infrastructure projects, private projects and SMEs in Korea. These banks are committed to support the financial strength of companies through direct equity investments although domestic companies generally have access to local funding as well as informal and secondary financial markets charging higher interest rates. Debentures are also used as a financing alternate, although slightly more expensive than bank financing. Finally, long-term debt is available from the Korea Development Bank (KDB), but generally for high priority industries.

In February 2013, the state-run Export-Import Bank of Korea announced that it will provide a total of KRW 74 trillion (USD 66 billion) in loans (KRW 50 trillion) and loan guarantees (KRW 24 trillion) to finance industrial activities and international development projects involving Korean companies amid a prolonged global downturn and the appreciation of the KRW. It will first finance large projects overseas related to engineering, procurement and construction (EPC), general construction, shipbuilding, and trade finance. This is a slight increase from the USD 62 billion executed in the previous year. It also set aside 45 percent of its total loan amount, or KRW 22.5 trillion (USD 20 billion), for SMEs to promote shared growth between large and small enterprises.

Bank of Korea: http://eng.bok.or.kr/

Commercial Service International Company Profile (ICP) www.export.gov/southkora/ICP

Country Limitation Schedule: http://www.exim.gov/tools/country/country_limits.html

Dun and Bradstreet: https://www.dnb.com/english/contactus/index.htm

Export-Import Bank of Korea: http://www.koreaexim.go.kr/en2/index.jsp

Financial Supervisory Commission: http://www.fsc.go.kr/eng/

Financial Supervisory Service: http://english.fss.or.kr/fss/en/main.jsp

Korea Investors Service: www.kisrating.com/eng/

Korean Appraisal Board: http://www.kab.co.kr/kab/home/eng/index.jsp

Korean Commercial Arbitration Board: www.kcab.or.kr/jsp/kcab_eng/index.jsp

KORUS FTA – Financial Services:
http://www.uskoreafta.org/sites/default/files/Financial-Services-KORUS.pdf

National Agricultural Cooperative Federation:
http://www.fsc.go.kr/eng/rl/list.jsp?menu=01&bbsid=BBS0060 and
http://www.nonghyup.com/eng/main/main.html

OPIC: http://www.opic.gov
Overseas Private Investment Corporation

Small Business Administration's (SBA) Office of International Trade:
http://www.sba.gov/oit/

Trade and Development Agency: http://www.tda.gov/

U.S. Agency for International Development: http://www.usaid.gov

USDA Commodity Credit Corporation: http://www.fsa.usda.gov/ccc/default.htm

Export-Import Bank of the United States: http://www.exim.gov

Country Limitation Schedule: http://www.exim.gov/tools/country/country_limits.html

Return to table of contents

Chapter 8: Business Travel

- Business Customs
- Travel Advisory
- Visa Requirements
- Telecommunications
- Transportation
- Language
- Health
- Local Time, Business Hours and Holidays
- Temporary Entry of Materials and Personal Belongings
- Web Resources

Business Customs   Return to top

U.S. businesses aiming to be successful in this dynamic and fascinating nation of 50 million should take time to learn about, and be cognizant of, some important facts.

Long history: Korea's over 10 thousand year history is one filled with dozens of rich dynasties and unfortunate conquests by rival Asian nations -- Japan and China. Japan first invaded Korea in 1592, followed by a Manchurian invasion in 1636, and another Japanese invasion from 1910 to 1945. The Republic of Korea, founded in 1948, soon experienced a civil war (1950-1953) which ended, in part, thanks to the arrival of U.S. military forces that have been present on the peninsula for 60 years. This history makes it important never to compare Korea to either Japan or China.

One of the world's most homogeneous societies, Korea is dominated by Confucian and Buddhist logic and traditions, which place great importance on age, rank, hierarchy and the value of one's community, collective society, or 'group think' -- all elements important in understanding how to navigate business in Korea. As important is the fact that any success in business is based upon the creation, establishment and maintenance of a solid relationship with your future business partners.

Post-Korean War: Korea in the 1950s and 1960s was one of the poorest countries in the world. Determined leaders gave economic/financial power to some privileged families, called *chaebols* (families that grew into multi-national, multi-sector industrial empires). The chaebols effectively and persistently combined their 'evolving sector expertise,' helped by a dense population in a geographically small area, into what is now a highly-respected and world-renown trillion-dollar economy driven by trade.

Today, Korea is known around the world for its popular and attractive white appliances, award-winning cars, smart phones and LED screens. It has a top-tier ranking in such diverse industries as ship building and the K-Pop "Korean Wave" culture called *hallyu,* which has captured fans worldwide, TV dramas, and attractive youth bands. Korea, hands-down, is also the most wired country in the world.

Korea hosted the Summer Olympics (1988), the Soccer World Cup (2002; along with Japan), the G-20 Leaders Summit (2010), and will host (2018) the Winter Olympics.

These major events, a source of pride and accomplishment, have intensified Korea's push to have a first-rate infrastructure, hospitality and transportation system.

The Han River Divides Seoul: Seoul is a modern, bustling, international city with all the first-class culinary, cultural and business amenities, variety and accommodations of any large metropolitan European or Asian city. The city is divided graciously and elegantly by the Han River and 27 bridges (all with a different architecture and feel; there were only three bridges crossing the Han in the 60s). After you arrive at the award-winning Incheon Airport, your hotel will be located either on the north side of the Han (where the airport and U.S. Embassy are located) or south of the Han. Traffic congestion, persistent and chronic, must be factored into arriving on-time for business appointments. In Korea, you should never be late. Instead, arrive 20 minutes early. That's the norm.

Other important business success *factoids*:

- Last names and titles: Always use Mr., Mrs., or any title (like Director) followed by the last name. Also appropriate is: Mr. LEE (last name, followed by the first name) Ji-hoon (two syllables of the first name); in this order.
- Business cards: Your business cards say a lot about you and your business and are extremely important in Asian and Korean cultures. Hand them out using both hands (thumbs at the top corners of your card) while giving a gentle and slight bow, while avoiding too much direct eye contact. Never put a newly-received business card away or in your back pocket. Rather, look at it for a moment and place it on the desk or table where you are meeting. Bilingual cards are best.
- Handshakes: Unlike the hard, firm Western-style handshake, a Korean's handshake may be a bit gentler.
- Cold calls are generally unacceptable and seen as culturally inappropriate and disrespectful.
- Negotiating: A rigid negotiating style does not work in Korea. Koreans interpret contracts *as loosely structured consensus statements,* broadly defining what has been negotiated/discussed, *but leaving room to permit flexibility and adjustment.* Koreans are subtle and effective negotiators. See Chapter 3 of this guide for additional insights into negotiating.
- While you learn Korean, these two important words should serve you:
  - Ann-yong-ha-sayo   – Hello and goodbye
  - Gam-sam-hap-nida   – Thank you

Travel Advisory   Return to top

Consult: U.S. State Department http://travel.state.gov/travel/cis_pa_tw/cis/cis_1018.html

Visa Requirements   Return to top

Visa Requirements for U.S. Citizens

- No visa is needed for a stay of up to 90 days
- A stay of over 90 days requires a visa

If planning to stay more than 90 days or for any purpose other than tourism or business, U.S. passport holders must obtain a visa prior to entering Korea. Americans coming to

Korea for activities such as employment, teaching English, or study must obtain a visa at a Korean embassy or consulate abroad.

For more information about Korean visa and entry requirements, please see the Korean Ministry of Justice's website at http://www.moj.go.kr/HP/ENG/index.do.

For information about visas to Korea, please see the Korean Ministry of Foreign Affairs and Trade website at:
http://www.mofa.go.kr/ENG/visa/application/index.jsp?menu=m_40_10

U.S. Companies that require travel of foreign businesspersons to the United States should be advised that security evaluations are handled via an interagency process. Visa applicants should go to the following links.

State Department Visa Website: http://travel.state.gov/visa/

U.S. Embassy Seoul Consular Section Website: http://www.asktheconsul.org

Telecommunications   Return to top

- Local calls
    - Dial 9 or 10 digit local phone number. There is no area code.
- International calls
    - Dial 00799 for a service that features: station-to-station calls, collect or reverse charge calls, and calls providing interpretation.
- Rent a mobile phone at kiosks at Incheon International Airport
    - And/or call these providers:
        - SK Telecom: 82-32-743-4011/4042
        - KT: 82-32-743-4018/4078
        - LG Telecom: 82-32-743-4001/4019
- Roaming and wireless internet
    - Consult your U.S. service provider to determine if your cell phone and plan will work in Korea. Beware of roaming and affiliated charges.
    - Most upscale hotels and coffee shops have wireless internet access.

Transportation   Return to top

- Consult: http://www.Koreapass.or.kr/en or call 1330 once in Korea

From Incheon International Airport to Downtown Seoul

- Train (AREX)
    - Direct railway links from the Incheon Airport to Seoul Station
    - Takes 43 minutes and runs every 30 minutes with no stops
    - Cost: KRW 14,300 (approx. USD 13)
    - Take the subway (inexpensive option) or taxi to your hotel from Seoul Station

- Airport Buses
    - Widely available to/from major cities in and around Seoul

- Located at the passenger arrival terminal level '1F'
- Cost: KRW 10,000-15,000 (approx. USD 10-15) depending on destination
- Consult: http://www.airport.kr/airport/traffic/bus/busList.iia?flag=E

- Taxis
  - Located at the passenger arrival terminal level '1F' between platforms 4D and 8C
    - Cost: KRW 60,000~80,000 (approx. USD 60-80). If overcharged, contact the airport authority (032-741-2422).

Other Transportation Recommendations

- Subway: Excellent, extremely clean and safe (nine lines)
  - Consult: seoulmetro.co.kr
  - Widely available to/from Seoul and Gyeonggi Province
  - Highly recommend **M-Pass** (only for foreigners)
    Consult: http://www.visitkorea.or.kr/ena/TR/TR_EN_5_1_4.jsp#Subway07
    - Covers large area around Seoul, other subway systems, and airport railroads
    - Purchase passes at tourism information centers at Incheon Airport
    - Cost: KRW10,000 for a one-day pass and KRW 59,500 for a week
      (plus a KRW 4,500 refundable deposit and KRW 500 non-refundable service charge)
  - Rush hour congestion: 7-9 am and 5-7pm, especially on lines 2 and 3
  - Pathfinder: http://traffic.visitkorea.or.kr/Lang/en/
  - Consult: http://www.visitkorea.or.kr/ena/TR/TR_EN_5_1_4.jsp

- Taxis
  - Cost based on distance and time and begin at KRW 2,400 (USD 2)
  - 20% cost increase between midnight and 4 am
  - No tipping required
  - Consult: http://asiaenglish.visitkorea.or.kr/ena/TR/TR_EN_5_2.jsp

- KTX (Korea Train Express)
  - Very clean, affordable and comfortable high-speed transportation to major cities throughout Korea. A trip from Seoul to Busan, for example, is 2.5 hours on KTX
  - Consult: http://ktx.korail.go.kr/eng/

Banking and Money

- Cards with the *Plus* and *Cirrus* logos are the most widely accepted in Korea
- CDs (Cash Dispenser Machines) only offer cash withdrawal services
  - CD machines located in: subway stations, bus terminals, and department stores
- ATMs offer withdrawals, deposits and fund transfers
  - ATM transactions require an account with a Korean bank

- Prominent Korean banks include: Korea Exchange Bank (KEB), Shinhan Bank, and Citibank
- Questions about ATM/CD machines: call 1330
- The Korean currency the 'won' is written with a large '₩' with a line through it or 'KRW.'

Travel

- Popular first-tier hotels in Seoul include: Hyatt, Hilton, JW Marriott, Conrad, Plaza, and Westin Chosun, although numerous other excellent hotels exist
- Street crime is almost non-existent, due to thousands of CCTV cameras and police present 24/7
- For affordable hotels consult: www.benikea.co.kr
- For Korea's weather consult: http://english.visitkorea.or.kr/enu/AK/AK_EN_1_1_2.jsp
- For Korea's currency consult: http://english.visitkorea.or.kr/enu/AK/AK_EN_1_5_4.jsp
- Korea electrical current operates at 220 volts
- Smoking is banned in thousands of parks, bus stops, subways, both indoors and outdoors. Personnel monitor and will fine violators USD80-100.

Language   Return to top

- Korean (Hangul) is the official and accepted business language
- Many Koreans in tourism and first-tier retail sales speak some English

Health   Return to top

- Dial 1339 for the Emergency Medical Information Center; trained medical personnel are on call 24 hours a day, 7 days a week
- Most hotels will assist you if you are sick. Call the front desk.
- You can purchase simple medications, such as Tylenol, Band-Aids, ointments and cold medication in pharmacies or in any general or "24-hour stores." For other medications, you will need a prescription from a doctor.
- International clinics at large prominent hospitals in Seoul include:
    - Severance Hospital (☎ 2-2228-5800):134, Sinchong-dong, Seodaemun-gu
    - Asan Medical Center (☎2-3010-5001): 388-1, Pungnap-dong, Songpa-gu, Seoul
    - Samsung Medical Center (☎2-3410-0200): 50, Irwon-dong, Gangnam-gu

For international health advisories related to Korea, please visit the CDC website at: http://wwwnc.cdc.gov/travel/destinations/south-korea.htm

Local Time, Business Hours, and Holidays   Return to top

Local Time Zone

- Korea is 13 hours ahead of EST and 14 hours ahead of EST during daylight savings. Korea does not switch to daylight savings time.
- Consult: http://www.timeanddate.com/worldclock/converter.html

Business Hours and Lunch Hours

- Offices and organizations: 9:00 am-6:00 pm; closed weekends and national holidays
- Banks: 9:00 am-4:00 pm; closed weekends and national holidays
- Department stores: 10:30 am-8:00 pm
- Koreans take lunch at essentially the same time, requiring luncheon reservations even for the smallest restaurants. You can avoid lines and crowds by taking lunch before 12:00 p.m. or after 1:00 p.m.

Holidays

Observed Korean Holidays – 2013

New Year's Day: January 1st	Memorial Day: June 6th
Lunar New Year's Day: February 9th – 11th	Liberation Day: August 15th
Independence Movement Day: March 1st	Chuseok Days: September 18th – 20th
Children's Day: May 5h	National Foundation Day: October 3rd
Buddha's Birthday: May 17h	Christmas Day: December 25th

- During Lunar New Year and Chuseok, all businesses and government offices are closed
- The U.S. Embassy is closed on both U.S. and Korean holidays
- Consult: http://www.timeanddate.com/calendar/?year=2013&country=70
-

Temporary Entry of Materials and Personal Belongings   Return to top

Prohibited Items
- Narcotics/illegal drugs of any kind
- Pornography and subversive material
- Products originating from Communist countries
- Explosives, ammunitions and weapons
- Rifles/sport guns (require permission from Korean Police prior to import, declaration upon arrival)
- Counterfeit money and coins

Articles in Excess of Duty Free Allowance

Coming into Korea consult:
http://www.airport.kr/iiacms/pageWork.iia?_scode=C1202010500

Returning to the U.S consult:
http://www.cbp.gov/xp/cgov/travel/vacation/ and http://www.tsa.gov/traveler-information

Web Resources   Return to top

Affordable hotels:	www.benikea.co.kr
Airport Bus:	http://www.airport.kr/airport/traffic/bus/busList.iia?flag=E
Benikea:	http://www.benikea.com
Coming to Korea:	http://www.airport.kr/iiacms/pageWork.iia?_scode=C1202010500
Currency:	http://english.visitkorea.or.kr/enu/AK/AK_EN_1_5_4.jsp
Holidays:	http://www.timeanddate.com/calendar/?year=2013&country=70
Incheon Int'l Airport:	http://www.airport.kr/eng/
Korean Emb. in U.S.:	http://usa.mofa.go.kr/english/am/usa/main/index.jsp
Korean Railroad:	http://www.korail.com/
KTX:	http://www.korail.com/
M Pass:	http://www.visitkorea.or.kr/ena/TR/TR_EN_5_1_4.jsp#Subway07
Returning to the U.S:	http://www.cbp.gov/xp/cgov/travel/vacation/
Subway Map:	http://traffic.visitkorea.or.kr/Lang/en/
Taxi:	http://asiaenglish.visitkorea.or.kr/ena/TR/TR_EN_5_2.jsp
Time Zone:	http://www.timeanddate.com/worldclock/converter.html
U.S. State Dept.:	http://travel.state.gov/travel/travel_1744.html
	and http://travel.state.gov/travel/cis_pa_tw/cis/cis_1018.html
U.S. Customs:	http://www.cbp.gov
U.S. Embassy Seoul Consular Section:	http://www.asktheconsul.org
Visas:	http://www.mofa.go.kr/ENG/visa/application/index.jsp?menu=m_40_10
Weather:	http://english.visitkorea.or.kr/enu/AK/AK_EN_1_1_2.jsp

Return to table of contents

Chapter 9: Contacts, Market Research and Trade Events

- Contacts
- Market Research
- Trade Events

Contacts Return to top

Go to the link below for useful contacts in Korea and the U.S.:

http://export.gov/southkorea/usefullinks/index.asp

Market Research Return to top

To view market research reports produced by the US Commercial Service please go to the following website at http://www.export.gov/mrktresearch/index.asp and click on Market Research Home.

Please note that these reports are only available to U.S. citizens and U.S. companies. Registration to the site is required and is free.

Trade Events Return to top

Please click on the link below for information on upcoming trade events.

http://www.export.gov/tradeevents/index.asp

http://export.gov/southkorea/tradeevents/index.asp

Return to table of contents

Chapter 10: Guide to Our Services

The President's National Export Initiative aims to double exports over five years by marshaling Federal agencies to **prepare U.S. companies to export successfully**, **connect them with trade opportunities** and **support them once they do have exporting opportunities**.

The U.S. Commercial Service offers customized solutions to help U.S. exporters, particularly small and medium sized businesses, successfully expand exports to new markets. Our global network of trade specialists will work one-on-one with you through every step of the exporting process, helping you to:

- Target the best markets with our world-class research
- Promote your products and services to qualified buyers
- Meet the best distributors and agents for your products and services
- Overcome potential challenges or trade barriers
- Gain access to the full range of U.S. government trade promotion agencies and their services, including export training and potential trade financing sources

To learn more about the Federal Government's trade promotion resources for new and experienced exporters, please click on the following link: www.export.gov

For more information on the services the U.S. Commercial Service offers to U.S. exporters, please click on the following link: (Insert link to Products and Services section of local buyusa.gov website here.)

U.S. exporters seeking general export information/assistance or country-specific commercial information can also contact the **U.S. Department of Commerce's Trade Information Center** at **(800) USA-TRAD(E).**

To the best of our knowledge, the information contained in this report is accurate as of the date published. However, **The Department of Commerce** does not take responsibility for actions readers may take based on the information contained herein. Readers should always conduct their own due diligence before entering into business ventures or other commercial arrangements. **The Department of Commerce** can assist companies in these endeavors.

Return to table of contents

www.ingramcontent.com/pod-product-compliance
Lightning Source LLC
Chambersburg PA
CBHW081328310526
45789CB00018B/2537